MOUNTAIN RECORD
OF ZEN TALKS

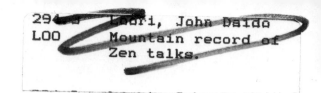

MOUNTAIN RECORD OF ZEN TALKS

John Daido Loori

EDITED BY
BONNIE MYOTAI TREACE

FOREWORD BY
HAKUYU TAIZAN MAEZUMI

SHAMBHALA
Boston & London
1988

SHAMBHALA PUBLICATIONS, INC.
HORTICULTURAL HALL
300 MASSACHUSETTS AVENUE
BOSTON, MA 02115

9 8 7 6 5 4 3 2 1

FIRST EDITION

Printed in the United States of America

Distributed in the United States by Random House and in Canada by Random House of Canada Ltd.

Library of Congress Cataloging-in-Publication Data
Loori, John Daido.
  Mountain record of Zen talks.
  1. Zen Buddhism—Doctrines. I. Title.
BQ9268.7.L66 1988 294.3'927   87-28605
ISBN 0-87773-445-3 (pbk.)

Cover photograph © 1988 by Robert Hansen-Sturm. The "mountains-and-rivers" design is the logo of Zen Mountain Monastery.
Several passages in chapter 9 were adapted from pp. 56–62 of *The Holy Teaching of Vimalakirti,* translated by Robert Thurman (University Park, Pa.: Pennsylvania State University Press, 1976). Reprinted by permission of the publisher.
The photographs on pages 39, 67, 101, and 145 are by John Daido Loori; on page 79 by Felicity Koen Zenie; and on page 165 by Stuart Soshin Gray. The brush paintings on pages 123 and 191 are by Gyokusei Jikihara; on page 6 by Kazuaki Tanahishi; on page 60 by Vo Dinh; and on p. 134 by Dosho Saikawa. All rights reserved.

To Hakuyu Taizan Maezumi Roshi
with inexpressible gratitude
for his teachings

CONTENTS

Foreword by Hakuyu Taizan Maezumi   *ix*

Editor's Preface   *xiii*

Acknowledgments   *xix*

Introduction   *1*

PART ONE: *Mountain Gate*

   1. The Search   7

   2. The Barrier Gate   *15*

   3. An Introduction to Zazen   *25*

   4. A Talk on *The Heart Sutra*   *31*

   5. Are You Awake?   *41*

   6. Ceaseless Practice   *47*

PART TWO: *Solitary Peak*

   7. Mountains and Rivers   *61*

   8. "The Sound of Rain"   *69*

   9. The Goddess's "Neither Male
      Nor Female"   *81*

  10. "Like a Dream"   *93*

  11. Accomplishing Buddha's Great Wisdom   *103*

  12. Transmission of the Light   *111*

  13. Painting Spring   *125*

PART THREE: *Valley Spirit*

  14. "Neither Difficult Nor Easy"   *135*

  15. Medicine and Sickness Cure Each Other   *147*

  16. Picking and Choosing, Coming
      and Going   *157*

  17. The Sacred Teachings of Work   *167*

CONTENTS

18. The Art of Seeing   *175*
19. Zen Mind, Well Mind   *183*
20. "Sages and Warriors Living Together"   *193*

Glossary   *203*
About Zen Mountain Monastery   *211*
Index   *213*

FOREWORD

OVER THE PAST FEW DECADES, various efforts to practice Zen by Americans have taken place in this country. Since the time I was sent from Japan to Zenshuji, a Soto Zen temple in Los Angeles, over thirty years have passed. During these years I have gone through different phases of my own practice. But from the very beginning, one of my major concerns has been the transmission of dharma to American practitioners. It is my deep pleasure and satisfaction to see this occurring.

As commonly understood, Zen was revealed by Shakyamuni Buddha in India and was transmitted to Korea, China, and Japan. Each country developed its own unique flavor of Zen according to the spiritual and cultural climate of each place and time. As a naturalized United States citizen for the past twenty-five years, I have observed this country's rich heritage, and it appears that the diversity of Zen practice will continue to flourish here with a distinctly American flavor. How this is accomplished will depend on the capacity and capabilities of the first generation of American-born teachers and on the cooperation and unity of the sangha, which is important to foster the succession of the dharma and to nourish its growth. With a sound basis in zazen, the diversity and possibilities of skillful means for revealing the dharma are boundless. In addition to the traditional methods, there are sure to be many innovative approaches to reach the spiritual needs of this time, place, and condition. In a way, it can be said that this is already occurring.

The charm of this book lies in the refreshing rearrangement of the classical koans and in their practical expression as they relate directly to the life of each of us. For example, instead of the traditional interpretations of koan collections such as *The Gateless Gate, The Blue Cliff Record,* and the *Book of Equanimity,* Daido Sensei restructures the koans from passages of Dogen Zenji's writings, the sutras, and records of the masters, and includes pointers and appreciatory verses from different sources.

It is generally understood that koan practice and shikantaza are opposing means of practice. However, I am more and more inclined to appreciate that they are basically the same. Case koans are used as the raft to reach the other shore, and yet the other shore, where such dichotomies are transcended, is always this shore right beneath our feet. This realization—the manifestation of koan as realized by Buddha—is the basis of Dogen Zenji's teaching that practice and enlightenment are one. In the Buddha's own expression of that realization, he said, "I and all sentient beings of the great earth have in the same moment attained the way." And when we do koan and shikantaza, this truth is manifested in the reality of each of our lives.

Zen Mountain Monastery is located in the Catskill Mountains in New York State. The facilities were originally built by Dominican monks and developed by Christian groups. Since Daido Sensei comes from a Catholic background and once intended to be a Catholic monk, his flexibility in adapting significant parts of the Christian monastic order and Zen monasticism is quite remarkable and convincing. The Christian and Buddhist dialogue occurring today is a wonderful activity. In addition, spending time together in the different monasteries to refresh and encourage one's own practice is a very significant endeavor. I hope that the readers of this book will find in it some significant contributions toward this end.

In 1987, Daido Sensei traveled to Japan for the *zuise* ceremony, during which he was the chief abbot of the two major Soto monasteries, Eiheiji and Sojiji, for a night. A dozen sangha members accompanied him. This event was a formal empowerment and serves to establish the credibility and continuity of the transmission from East to West. Like the transmission of the dharma to Asia, it is my hope that here in the West the roots of the dharma will go deep and be established well in Western culture, so that it may continue its endless enfoldment.

Hakuyu Taizan Maezumi
ZEN MOUNTAIN CENTER
SAN JACINTO MOUNTAINS,
CALIFORNIA
SUMMER 1987

EDITOR'S PREFACE

THE CHAPTERS in this collection were first presented by John Daido Loori Sensei as Dharma Discourses at Zen Mountain Monastery, and later appeared in the monastery's quarterly journal, *Mountain Record*. Over the years we have had many requests for reprints of the talks and have so often made copies for distribution that it became obvious that the time had come to publish these discourses as a collection. We offer this present selection as a beginning, with future editions to follow.

Dharma Discourse involves a very special kind of speaking and hearing, and because of that, some opening remarks may be helpful.

Before each Dharma Discourse we announce that the talk about to be given is very different from an ordinary lecture, that it speaks to the heart, not the intellect. We remind those present that it is important to listen as if one were the only person in the room, that one should hear the words as if they were spoken for oneself alone. The setting in which a Dharma Discourse is given is also important to appreciate, because it profoundly affects how the words are received. The Zen teacher speaks from the very center of his being, presenting not descriptions of reality, but words that arise directly out of a deep personal experience of the ground of being itself. In this sense, receiving a Dharma Discourse is completely different from getting information about something, its whole point being that you, the listener, have the experience yourself.

Daido Sensei has called Dharma Discourses "dark to the mind but radiant to the heart": they require that we open ourselves to what initially may seem an intentionally confusing and frustrating way of using language. At the monastery, Dharma Discourse takes place in a context of intensive Zen meditation (*zazen*), which works to open that space in the center of our own being, allowing the words to penetrate. Because reading is essentially solitary, the intimacy of heart-to-heart, mind-to-mind communication that characterizes Dharma Discourse may in a way be even easier. Please read the words that follow with your heart, giving them your full attention, letting go for the time you devote to this book all the thoughts and analyses that are our habit of mind. One of the dangers of words is that we think we have something once we know its name. The practice of reading or hearing a Dharma Discourse lies not in the acquisition of names and descriptions, but in the direct and personal experience of Buddha-mind. Our job as listeners or readers is not to put ourselves in the way of that.

Dharma Discourse generally deals with a Zen *koan,* a seemingly paradoxical statement or question that challenges our understanding of who we are, what the nature of the self is, and what the activity of our life expresses. There are currently available in English translation many commentaries on classical Zen koans by Japanese, Chinese, and Korean masters, which for the last twenty years or so have provided American students access to the way Zen study has been brought to life through the lineage of realized teachers that began with Shakyamuni Buddha 2,500 years ago. We are only now entering a time when first-generation American masters are speaking directly to American students in our native idiom.

The presentations in this volume are part of this shift, an important transition for which we owe a great debt of gratitude both to the teachers who traveled here from Asia, embracing a language and a culture very different from their own, and to the first-generation dharma heirs who made the living transmission of Zen to America possible. Daido Sensei received dharma sanction from Hakuyu

Taizan Maezumi Roshi, lineage holder in both the Rinzai and Soto schools of Japanese Zen, and a teacher dedicated to the subtle and elegant depths of Master Dogen's teaching. Due to his training with Maezumi Roshi, Daido Sensei's teaching expresses a unifying of the traditional schism often identified between Rinzai "koan Zen" and the emphasis on silent introspection in the Soto school, as well as a deep resonance with the beauty and liveliness of language that Dogen's words expound. The training at Zen Mountain Monastery revealed through these talks is a daily life that takes up Zen monastic tradition in a uniquely American context. Zazen is emphasized, koan study is an important part of the training, and all of it is engaged in by a cross-section of practitioners that includes both monks and lay people.

The discourse always moves in the direction of the audience present at the time—responding to the circumstances and needs of the students listening. Because the practitioners at Zen Mountain Monastery have such an amazing array of professional and personal interests, the talks use an equally dimensional array of skillful means to point the way. Artists are met with talks on "The Art of Seeing," physicians and psychologists with "Zen Mind, Well Mind." Martial arts practitioners are presented with "Sages and Warriors Living Together," and professionals and householders with "The Sacred Teachings of Work." As the reader of these talks will find, the gift of having the dharma spoken in this fresh, ordinary way, by a teacher who shares the conditioning of the same culture we've come up in, creates an opening into how we live our life, a wonderful way to turn around the way we use our mind.

In Part One of this collection, "Mountain Gate," the way practice begins for a student is explored, beginning with questioning, the bubbling up or bursting out of doubt that motivates us to look at what our life is, and the initial step into taking responsibility for what we find. The grit and bones of how to enter the Way, begin zazen, hear the teachings, and develop student mind and an active appreciation for the depth and breadth that a life of practice entails are all taken up in these first six chapters. In a way, these first chapters are about the beginning of training, but the distinction is also arbitrary—the beginning level, as well as the more advanced teachings that follow all happen simultaneously. From these first chapters, one of the most exciting characteristics of Daido Sensei's teaching becomes evident in that koans and koan study immediately explode out of their traditional boundaries. Not only are the classic collections (*The Gateless Gate, The Blue Cliff Record, The Transmission of the Light,* and the *Book of Equanimity*) used as points of departure, but also the record of Layman P'ang, the *Vimalakirti Sutra, The Heart Sutra,* and Dogen's *Shobogenzo* are developed, as Daido Sensei takes up a phrase from them, adds a pointer and a verse, and then provides a modern commentary that speaks to our daily practice. It's a broad look at what a koan can be, dynamic with the realization that the records of the masters are chock-full of the reflective, resonating turning of the mind that koan study provides when really engaged.

Accomplishing the "Solitary Peak" is the cumulative step in many religious traditions, reaching the mountain top's clear vista, the vast and inexpressible mystical experience of enlightenment. In the seven chapters that comprise Part Two, this experience itself is explored. That enlightenment is not the domain only of sages and holy men, but a possibility for each of us—and indeed our birthright—is the basis of the monastery's daily training program, and brought to light with striking clarity in chapters such as "The Goddess's 'Neither Male Nor Female.'" For the first time, Zen training is happening in a country where egalitarian principles are a fundamental value; that women and men, monk and lay practitioner, are training together, realizing and manifesting the Buddha Way in their lives, is a natural and celebrated expression in these talks.

In our practice, however, the path does not end on the

mountain's solitary peak, but needs to manifest itself directly in the world we live in. Part Three addresses the importance of the continuous and lucid actualizing of what has been realized. But where do you go when you've reached the top of the mountain? Back down the other side, back into "the marketplace." This is the journey taken up in the seven final chapters that make up the "Valley Spirit" selection of talks. At Zen Mountain Monastery, the training program specifically involves seven areas or "gates" of self-study: zazen, zen study with the teacher, liturgy, art practice, body practice, academic study, and work practice. In "The Sacred Teachings of Work," readers will see how livelihood, our means of making a living, and the basic way we do the things we do become places to bring the Buddha-mind to life. Many people new to Zen are surprised by its hard-working spiritedness and attentiveness to the details of how a carrot is sliced, a saw sharpened—always the proving ground of spiritual life is the moment itself, whether that moment is spent on the pillow doing zazen or in the garden thinning the asparagus. Also, due to Sensei's background as a prominent photographer and visual artist, the "self expressed in self-expression" has become a powerful part of his teaching at the monastery, as "The Art of Seeing" chapter reveals.

I hope that the work of bringing the spoken word into written form in this collection is as invisible as possible, and apologize for any instances where my editorial hand may have gotten in the way of the intimacy in the dharma that Daido Sensei creates as he speaks. I hope that if you first encounter the Buddha Way through these words, the practice does become your own, and the monastery a source of nourishment and support. Again, please sit quietly with these words, and take advantage of the fact that they are offered for no one but yourself.

I deeply appreciate the opportunity to give my time to this incredible work, ever skillfully created by my teacher and the teachers before him, to point the way. It is my sincere hope that the larger sangha of readers enjoy these words and are as encouraged by them as those who were at the monastery when the talks were first offered.

Bonnie Myotai Treace, Editor
Mountain Record

ACKNOWLEDGMENTS

T HE AUTHOR wishes to acknowledge that without several excellent English translations of basic Buddhist texts this work would not have been possible. Of particular value were Thomas Cleary and J. C. Cleary's translation of *The Blue Cliff Record,* 2 vols. (Boulder & London: Shambhala Publications, 1977), Zenkei Shibayama's translation and commentary in *Zen Comments on the Mumonkan* (San Francisco: Harper & Row, 1984), and Koun Yamada's translation of *The Gateless Gate* (Los Angeles: Center Publications, 1980). I am also deeply grateful for Robert A. F. Thurman's translation, *The Holy Teaching of Vimalakirti* (University Park: Pennsylvania State University Press, 1976), which was adapted for the discussion in chapter 9; Kosen Nishiyama and John Stevens's authoritative translation of Dogen Zenji's master work, the *Shobogenzo* (Briarcliff Manor, N.Y.: Japan Publications, 1975); and Carl Bielefeldt's beautiful translation of *The Mountains and Rivers Sutra* in Michael C. Tobias and Harold Drasdo, *Mountain Spirit* (New York: Overlook Press, 1983). Katsuki Sekida's translation, *Two Zen Classics: Mumonkan and Hekiganroku* (New York: Weatherhill, 1977); the translation of Sengstan's *Verses on the Faith Mind* by Richard B. Clark (Bakersfield, Calif.: Universal Press); and *The Recorded Sayings of Layman P'ang,* translated by Ruth Fuller Sasaki, Yoshitaka Iriya, and Dana R. Fraser (New York: Weatherhill, 1971) were also invaluable. At times where several translations of the same work were available in English, composite translations were used to clarify the point being made. The translation used of Dogen Zenji's essay "Painting Spring" is an unpublished in-house document of the Zen Community of New York, and the translations of *The Heart Sutra* and *The Transmission of the Lamp* are unpublished in-house documents of the Zen Center of Los Angeles.

I wish to express my appreciation to the staff of Zen Mountain Monastery for their help in preparing the manuscript, particularly *Mountain Record* editor Bonnie Myotai Treace, without whose editorial skills this work would never have materialized as a book.

Mountain Record

INTRODUCTION

SINCE ITS EARLIEST BEGINNINGS, the practice of Zen has always been characterized as:

A special transmission outside the scriptures
with no reliance on words and letters.
A direct pointing to the human mind,
and the realization of Buddhahood.

With zazen (sitting meditation) as its basis, the introspection of the koan is one of Zen's most effective skillful means of "direct pointing." The colorful and apparently paradoxical encounters between Zen adepts which form the basis of the classical koans have intrigued Westerners for many years. I use the term "apparently paradoxical" because in reality there are no paradoxes; paradox exists in the language we use to describe reality. In the direct and intimate experience of reality itself, there are no paradoxes.

Koans and koan collections are becoming increasingly available in the West. New translations and studies in English and other Western languages have made koans much more accessible, so that the word *koan* itself has come into familiar usage, even among those not actively doing Zen training. Much has been written about koans in terms of their value as subjects of philosophical and intellectual study. There is no question that koans are of great scholarly value—they contain a goldmine of information on the philosophy and history, the morality and ethics, and the language and poetry of Zen. But the primary value of a koan, and indeed its uniqueness, lies in its use as a vehicle for spiritual realization.

1

In a Dharma Discourse, the koan is taken up as a vehicle of Zen training and practice. Training and practice are by definition concerned with doing: to practice is to do. To train the mind with a koan is to do, to put every bit of energy and attention you have into realizing it personally, rather than becoming involved in its philosophical or intellectual aspects. Practicing a koan is not a matter of understanding or believing, but rather of direct realization. To realize a koan is to *be* it with the whole body and mind; to be it with the whole body and mind is to forget the self.

In actual practice, the koan becomes the object of one's concentration, the object of one's being. To work with a koan is to go beyond the words and ideas and experience the direct reality itself. Because of this, koans tend to frustrate the intellectual process, and that frustration is an important part of koan study. Until we've exhausted the possibility that we can "figure out" the koan, we keep the intellect going. But koans cannot be realized through linear, discursive thought; they involve the direct and intuitive aspect of our consciousness. In the West our process of education is directed primarily toward developing and refining linear, discursive thought, said to be centered in the left hemisphere of the brain. And indeed, linear, discursive thought plays an important role in our understanding of the universe and our functioning in the world. We should realize, however, that this represents only half of the potential of human consciousness. There is another half—that which is direct and intuitive. It is this direct and intuitive aspect of consciousness that is at the heart of all of the great advances of the human race, not only our spiritual and artistic advances, but those of science and technology as well.

Through the process of working with the koan, we begin slowly to open up that other aspect of consciousness and learn to trust its functioning. Working with the koan begins to churn up many of the things we have been suppressing for years—bringing them up into surface consciousness where they can be acknowledged and released. It's necessary to empty oneself out in order to "see" a koan, but you can't empty yourself out as long as you continue to hold on to the baggage of concepts, positions, and ideas. A single thought separates us from the koan. And, of course, the emptying process in and of itself is very refreshing. It makes us free, and able to probe the depths of the koan.

A single koan can be a multilayered experience, each layer to be thoroughly chewed, swallowed, digested, and assimilated into every cell of our being, like a full-course dinner, from appetizer to dessert. Sometimes we only see the main point of the koan and miss the fullness of the other layers. It's like only tasting the appetizer. And dealing only with the philosophical and intellectual implications is kind of like reading the menu and completely missing the meal. Coupled with a pointer and a verse, the koan becomes a virtual feast of spiritual training.

Many koan collections and koan training systems have evolved over the centuries. Each one was intended to fulfill the needs of the particular time and place in which it was developed, yet at the same time we can see in all of them a universality of the questions that they pose. Understanding the ultimate nature of reality transcends any time or place. A koan is much more than words and ideas—it's a direct pointing, a revelation of spiritual realization that is paralleled in every "bible" of human experience.

Most of the work with a koan takes place alone while sitting zazen, because in reality there's nothing anyone can give us. There's nothing that we lack. Each one of us is perfect and complete, lacking nothing. That's why it is said that there are no Zen teachers and nothing to teach. But this truth must be realized by each one of us. Great faith, great doubt, and great determination are three essentials for that realization. It is a boundless faith in oneself and in the ability to realize oneself and make oneself free, and a deep and penetrating doubt which asks: Who am I? What is life? What is truth? What is God? What is reality? This great faith and great doubt are in dynamic tension with each other, and work to provide the real cutting edge of koan practice. When great faith and great doubt are also accompanied by great determination (the determination of "Seven times knocked down, eight times get up"), we have at our disposal the power necessary to break through our delusive way of thinking and realize the full potential of our lives.

The constant pointing that is the nature of Dharma Discourse is the awkward attempt of Zen teachers to assist students in realizing themselves. There is no correct "answer" to a koan. Seeing it is a state of consciousness in which our usual reference system has been abandoned and the thing itself is seen directly and intimately. This intimacy transforms our way of seeing ourselves and the universe. Once realized it is no longer possible to live our lives in the old way.

These chapters represent one experience of these koans, and as such they remain dead until you, the reader, make them your own, bring them to life in the moment-to-moment reality of your own existence. At that time, these words, having fulfilled their meager function, should be thrown away, so that the spiritual journey may continue as it is and always has been from the beginningless beginning—boundless and unhindered.

PART ONE
Mountain Gate

1

THE SEARCH

RECENTLY, after Zen painter Gyokusei Jikihara Sensei had spent some time in residency at Zen Mountain Monastery, he left as a gift a series of his ten Oxherding Pictures. The ten Oxherding Pictures correspond to specific stages of Zen practice. In a sense it is rather arbitrary to take anything as vivid and alive as Zen training and break it into chunks and attach labels to it, arranging it in a linear sequential order. And an individual's development in the practice does not always follow this pattern. But the guidelines expressed through the images of the Oxherding Pictures give us a perspective on what our training is about, and what it is we must do in order to progress along the Way.

Kakuan, a master of ancient times, gave a pointer and poem on each of the ten pictures. In the first picture Master Kakuan's poem for the image says: *The search for the bull—it has never been lost; what need is there to search?* The search is the first stage. This first step in spiritual unfolding has its parallel in virtually every religious journey. It was part of the journey of Moses, Christ, and Muhammad. Shakyamuni Buddha himself spent many years seeking the answer to the question of human suffering, old age, and death. The search by its very nature is wide, radiating in the ten directions. We may spend years constantly seeking, wandering the face of the earth—to India, Japan, China—trying one thing after another. We check out the ther-

THE SEARCH IS THE FIRST STAGE.

apies, encounter groups, New Age workshops. We investigate Hinduism, Catholicism, Buddhism. We look to philosophy, psychology—East Coast, West Coast. Yet, as the poem says, *It has never been lost; what need is there to search?* Where can we possibly look? What is there that is outside the self? How can it be lost?

Master Kakuan's pointer: *In the pasture of this world, I endlessly push aside the tall grasses in search of the bull. Following unnamed rivers, lost upon the interpenetrating paths of distant mountains, my strength failing and vitality exhausted, I cannot find the bull, I only hear the locust chirring through the forests.*

The bull represents the self, the eternal principal of life, truth in action. The ten bulls are images of the sequential steps in the realization of one's true nature. Kakuan's comment: *The bull has never been lost. What need is there to search? Only because of separation from my true nature, I fail to find him. In the confusion of the senses I lose even his tracks. Far from home, I see many crossroads, but which way is the right one, I do not know. Greed, fear, good and bad entangle me.* At this stage of practice, we begin to acknowledge the fact that life is pain—the same acknowledgment that the Buddha made. We awaken to the fact that there is something we need to know. The search is on.

In Zen practice itself, the search begins when the student starts meditation. The student begins the process of searching for the self, examining the self, studying the self. To study the Buddha Way is to study the self. The imagery of Kakuan's pointer and commentary translates into day-to-day reality, day-to-day practice. It is the same practice, whether we are talking about a lay practitioner, a monk, or a nun. It is the training of body, mind, and spirit. In the process of training we come to realize that these are not three separate things.

At Doshinji (the temple name of Zen Mountain Monastery), we have broken up the training into seven different areas of training: zazen, Zen study, academic study, liturgy practice, art practice, body practice, and work practice. In

WHAT IS THERE THAT IS OUTSIDE THE SELF?

WE ACKNOWLEDGE THE FACT THAT LIFE IS PAIN.

each of the ten stages there is a different level of accomplishment in each of the seven areas. The body is trained through the martial arts or their equivalent, the mind through Zen study and academic study, the spirit through zazen and liturgy. That training in body, mind, and spirit is actualized on a daily basis through our art practice, training positions, and work practice.

In the first stage of practice, the major emphasis is on zazen, particularly working with posture, becoming aware of the breath, and developing the *hara*. The hara is not only the physical center of the body, but the spiritual center as well. Both novices and more advanced students do three hours a day of zazen—four hours a day during the three-month intensive training period. Each month an intensive meditation retreat (*sesshin*) is held. Meditation is the core of our practice. Our activity—in body practice, liturgy practice, academic study, training positions, work practice—all arises from the stillness that develops in the *zendo*. In zazen we look at the self, study it, begin to understand how our own mind works. Bit by bit, *samadhi*—single-pointedness of mind—develops; we learn how to take all our scattered energy and bring it into focus. Zen study is supported by Dharma talks, interview, and Dharma Combat, which are directed toward helping the student gain a clearer understanding of the nature of the self.

Academic study provides a historical and theoretical perspective and familiarizes the student with the techniques of Zen practice. Most people have no idea of how Zen training works. For most of us it is unlike anything we have ever experienced. There is no relationship whatsoever to what goes on in universities. It is not the same as an apprenticeship. It is not the same kind of training that goes on in other seminaries and monasteries in America. Usually it is necessary to start from scratch to develop an appreciation of the method of Zen, the techniques that are used, and how the teaching takes place, so that the student

IN ZAZEN WE BEGIN TO UNDER-STAND HOW OUR OWN MIND WORKS.

can learn to be open and receptive and begin to appreciate the subtleties of this practice.

Liturgy practice involves attending all of the services, learning the chants, and developing chanting skills. The student learns to chant from the hara, to blend with everyone else, and develops a sense of oneness with the Sangha as our voices come together. Body, breath, and mind are brought into harmony in liturgy practice. It is an extension of meditation practice; we carry through the same focus, the same concentration, into the realm of activity.

BODY, BREATH, AND MIND ARE BROUGHT INTO HARMONY.

Art practice has been traditionally associated with Zen, especially during the Sung period in China and the Kamakura period in Japan. It survives now mainly at monasteries or training centers of the Obaku Zen sect, such as Jikihara Sensei's temple, where Nenga painting is part of Zen training. At Doshinji, students are introduced to Zen arts in the context of Zen practice. Through reading, study, and individual art practice, students begin to see the relationship of self-realization to art and the creative process. They are looking in a new way at what self-expression is all about, at what the self is that is being expressed in self-expression. During the year the monastery holds retreats that give resident and visiting students an opportunity to study with masters in the traditional Zen arts. Retreats with these masters, whose art is firmly rooted in Zen practice, are forming a connection between classical Zen art and a new Zen art that is being developed by western Zen practitioners. One purpose of the Zen Arts Training Program is to provide the catalyst, to create the conditions for that to happen.

In body practice, the student is encouraged to engage in one of the martial arts, such as Kung Fu, Karate, or Aikido, although other forms of body practice are also used. The relationship of Zen practice to the martial arts dates back to Shaolin Monastery, where the martial arts were considered an important aspect of Zen training. Since then the practice has gradually died out. In introducing the martial arts at Doshinji, we treat them as an extension of Zen training.

Training positions in the first three or four months, when a student is still getting oriented, are usually simple jobs such as kitchen cleanup or helping to set up for morning liturgy. In the second stage of practice, students are asked to fill zendo and Buddha Hall training positions, which involve greater responsibility. In training positions, students learn to manifest Zen practice in activity, to meet demands which become greater as they advance in training.

Work practice is an important training opportunity. In daily tasks at the monastery or in the marketplace, students are expected to develop the ability to keep their attention focused in the midst of distractions. Work practice involves learning how to work with other people, how to deal with negative emotions and attitudes, how to communicate yet keep silence as much as possible. It involves learning to be receptive, reliable, efficient, and organized. As in other areas of training, demands and responsibilities increase as students progress. When they reach a certain point of maturity in zazen, their work, their lives, and everything they do develops an equivalent clarity and integrity.

WORK PRACTICE INVOLVES LEARNING TO DEAL WITH NEGATIVE EMOTIONS.

As the practice evolves and we become clearer, the demands made on us increase. In the process of training, we begin to see that our ability, our potential, is far greater than we had thought. Many of us think we have gone as far as we can, but there are no limits to what we can do. Possibilities are boundless. The only thing that limits us is ourselves—our ideas, positions, and opinions.

THE ONLY THING THAT LIMITS US IS OURSELVES.

Although the program I have described is specifically designed for full-time seminarian training, it is just as applicable to anyone living and practicing away from the monastery. The process may take longer, but nonresidents who have really intense commitment progress as fast or faster than some people in resident training. To strength-

11

en and support their practice, nonresident students visit the monastery often and take part in sesshins and special intensive training retreats. In the beginning it is very easy to become romantically involved with Zen practice. If we begin by engaging in practice in a romantic way—taking the posture of the Buddha, being carried away by the fragrance of incense, the robes, the ceremony, the exotic sounds of blocks, bells, and gongs—it is okay. But sooner or later it wears thin. If there is not strong determination, great faith and great doubt underneath the romantic notions, the practice begins to deteriorate. We call it the three-month syndrome, after which the romance ends and the student settles down to the real work.

What is happening in this stage of practice is that we really begin to look at what causes pain, what causes greed, anger, and ignorance. We come to realize that it has to do WE ARE with separation. Because of separation we are caught up in CAUGHT UP the three poisons of greed, anger, and ignorance (delu- IN THE sion). When we realize that there is no separation between THREE self and others, no separation between inside and outside, POISONS OF our way of perceiving the world and ourselves is complete- GREED, ly transformed. Before this point is reached, as Master ANGER, AND Kakuan's poem says, *greed, fear, good and bad entangle me.* IGNORANCE. We are completely locked into the conditioning of our life. What we are actually dealing with when we sit and really look at ourselves is twenty, thirty, forty, fifty years of continuous conditioning that have created the illusion of self, of a separate entity. Until we really look at that and understand how it is functioning, we cannot get through it and on to the stages beyond. So the practice at this first stage, the stage of the "search," is letting go, making ourselves empty and receptive.

Far from home I see many crossroads, but which one is the right one I do not know. Zazen gets us oriented so that there is no question about the path that we must take. When we clearly see it, we raise the bodhi mind, and the path is entered. The first stage takes a different length of time, depending on individual *karma,* on what each person brings into the practice—on what each one of us is holding on to. But regardless of where we start from or how long we've practiced, until we've raised the bodhi mind—the clear aspiration for enlightenment—we haven't stepped onto that path. At that point we realize that we are already on the Way, and this is where the real work begins.

It has never been lost. What need is there to search? This line is based on what Shakyamuni Buddha said after his own enlightenment: "Isn't it wonderful! All sentient beings have the Buddha nature." That is, they are already enlightened. You may say, so why should we even bother? To understand intellectually what the Buddha said does not do anything. It is just another idea. When you believe it you have another belief system. But when you realize it in your own life, the realization is transformative. You can never live your life in the old way. *It has never been lost: what need is there to search?* comes from the point of view of that realization. In this first stage we do what the Buddha did. When he finally rejected asceticism, took the milk that was offered to him and nourished his body, and sat in zazen under the Bodhi Tree, he entered the path. It is the same path that we enter when we finally recognize that this is the way to self-realization. The search ends as we step onto the path of the Buddhas, clearly marked for us by twenty-five centuries of teachers transmitting the living dharma from mind to mind. Each one of us should appreciate how fortunate we are to live in a time and in a place where it is possible to follow this wonderful path. The only way we can express our gratitude for these teachers is by practicing diligently and accomplishing the Way ourselves.

THE SEARCH ENDS AS WE STEP ONTO THE PATH OF THE BUDDHAS.

2
The Barrier Gate

INSIDE THE MAIN GATE OF EIHEIJI, the temple founded by Master Dogen in 1244 and one of Soto Zen's two main temples, are two wooden plaques inscribed with Chinese characters to inform all who seek entry that "Only those concerned with the question of life and death need enter here" and "Those not completely concerned with this question have no reason to enter this gate." People are attracted to Zen practice for many reasons. Motivations and aspirations range from mere curiosity at one extreme to a deep spiritual quest at the other. The signs at Eiheiji's entrance gate make clear the function of the practice there and are an attempt to bring the aspirations and motivations of those entering in accord with the purpose of the monastery. It is common practice in many clusters to present entrance barriers or requirements not only for religious institutions but secular institutions as well. Throughout the history of Zen monasticism and Zen arts training, the barrier to entry has always functioned. Many of the koans studied in Zen emphasize the importance of the proper state of mind required for penetrating the "gateless barriers" of the various masters.

Master Dogen taught that "to study the Buddha Way is to study the self. To study the self is to forget the self, and to forget the self is to be enlightened by the ten thousand things." For most of us, the path of studying the self and forgetting the self is one of the most difficult encounters

"ONLY THOSE CONCERNED WITH THE QUESTION OF LIFE AND DEATH NEED ENTER HERE."

15

we will experience in our lifetime. The self is elusive, steeped in years of deep conditioning; it is specifically programmed not to be forgotten. Because of this, a deep spiritual drive needs to be at work if there is to be any hope at all of penetrating the barriers encountered in studying the self. We set up entrance barriers to test the perseverance and determination of the prospective student. Some of these barriers are formal entrance requirements; others are part of the encounter with the teacher and part of the process of establishing the spiritual training relationship necessary for the teaching to really begin.

Bodhidharma sat facing the wall. The Second Ancestor, who had been standing in the snow throughout the night, cut off his own arm and said, "Your disciple's mind is not yet at peace. I beg you, my teacher, please give it peace."

Bodhidharma said, "Bring the mind to me and I will set it at rest."

The Second Ancestor said, "I have searched for the mind and it is finally unobtainable."

Bodhidharma said, "There, I have thoroughly set it at rest for you."

The words don't really get at what is going on in this koan. There are two important things for us to see here. One is the point of the koan itself, which has to do with the nature of peace of mind, and another has to do with the barrier of entering the Mountain Gate, of preparing to "scale the Silver Mountain" called realization. I remember a year or two ago when a monk from another *sangha* was studying with us. He had been working on this koan for a very long time, and by the middle of a sesshin he was obviously very deep into it. Working on a koan is not like working on a riddle; it's not just something that you run around in your mind. It is specifically designed to short-circuit the whole intellectual process. You can't really see a koan by linear, sequential thought; you have to resort to another aspect of mind. When he tried to talk to me about the koan, he couldn't speak but just burst out crying

WORKING ON A KOAN IS NOT LIKE WORKING ON A RIDDLE.

and sobbing. I waited for him to quiet down enough to begin speaking. Finally he sobbed out, "How could he have possibly done this? How could he let that man stand in the snow until he was so desperate that he cut off his arm!" Now, this monk was the koan itself. He had identified totally with it. He still hadn't penetrated it, but he was well on the way to understanding it. It was no longer an intellectual exercise for him. His whole body and mind were totally enveloped in it. His question came from the core of his being, as did the question of the Second Ancestor.

In one of the classic koan collections, *The Transmission of the Lamp*, there is a more detailed description of what took place on that day. It says, "Shinko [the Second Ancestor] went over to Shaolin, and day and night he beseeched Bodhidharma for instruction. The master always sat in zazen facing the wall and paid no attention to him." Shinko waited outside saying, "May I enter?" and the master ignored him. "Please, may I enter? May I study with you?" and Bodhidharma still ignored him. Then, on the evening of December 9, there was a very heavy snowstorm. It snowed all day and all night. Shinko just stood there without moving. Toward daybreak the snow was waist-high, and still he stood, unmoving, waiting to be recognized by Bodhidharma.

Finally Bodhidharma turned and looked at him, "You've been standing in the snow a long time. What is it that you're seeking?"

Shinko, in bitter tears, said, "I beseech you, O Master, with your compassion, pray, open your gate of the dharma, and save all us beings."

Bodhidharma said, "The incomparable truth of the Buddha can only be attained by eternally striving, practicing what cannot be practiced, and bearing the unbearable. How can you with your little virtue, little wisdom, and your easy and self-conceited mind aspire to attain the true teaching? It's only so much labor lost." Shinko secretly took out a sharp knife, cut off his left arm and placed it in

"OPEN YOUR GATE OF THE DHARMA."

17

front of the master. Bodhidharma, recognizing his dharma caliber, said, "Buddhas, when they first seek after the truth, give no heed to their bodies for the sake of the dharma. You have now cut off your arm before me. I see the sincerity of your seeking."

Shinko asked, "Is it possible to listen to the Buddhadharma?"

The master replied, "The Buddhadharma cannot be attained by following others. One has to see directly into his own nature."

Then Shinko said, "My mind is not yet at peace. I beg you, my teacher, please give it peace."

"MY MIND IS NOT YET AT PEACE. I BEG YOU, PLEASE GIVE IT PEACE."

In order to appreciate this koan, we must begin by appreciating the state of mind of Master Shinko. This wasn't just some experience in personal growth. It was his whole life. There was nothing else in the whole universe that mattered more to him more than realizing his peace of mind. He was on the edge of his life, desperate, open, and receptive. It's very similar to read the accounts of some of the great Western mystics—Francis of Assisi, John of the Cross, Theresa of Avila. In their mystical searching, they also encountered this struggle. It is, indeed, a struggle to go deep into one's self, beyond all the conditioning of our parents, culture, education, and peers, and directly experience that ground of being, the reality of our existence. "Your disciple's mind is not yet at peace. I beg you, my teacher, please give it peace." The forms and expressions of asking may differ, yet isn't this the search that every one of us must make? Through all ages, human beings have made this search, some even at the cost of their lives. There's no account of how many of these monks on the road died of starvation, were devoured by wild animals, or killed by thieves as they carried on their great search. It's not just a personal desire entertained by Shinko over a thousand years ago. Zen Buddhism, like any religion in the world, must find the reason for its existence in guiding those who pursue the truth. By making this search, one is finally led to the realization of the nature of the self, the nature of true peace. Those who have never wept all night in a struggle of despair can never appreciate the struggle of this man. Master Shibayama quotes a Western theologian who once said, "You who have not spent sleepless nights in suffering and tears, who do not know the experience of being unable to swallow even a piece of bread, the grace of God will never reach you." *My mind is not yet at peace, I beg you, my teacher, please give it peace.* This is what we call the Great Doubt. Only those who break through the extremity of this sheer darkness can have the great joy of being true master of their own existence.

The barrier of entering into practice is sometimes difficult to understand because many religions are kind of evangelistic, bringing people into the "flock," saving souls. That is not our way; in fact, we do exactly the opposite by creating barriers to entry. Only those who can pass through those barriers have any hope of accomplishing themselves. The journey is that difficult. It requires that much commitment. That's why we use the metaphor of the lioness who pushes her cubs off the edge of the cliff and will only raise those who can climb back up to where she is. It seems very cruel. The poor runt of the litter is not going to make it. Only the strong ones are going to make it. The key to appreciating this koan is to understand the difference between "doing good" and the functioning of compassion. With doing good, there is sentimentality. In a sense, compassion is the act of being selfish, because everything is nothing but yourself, and you've realized it with your whole body and mind. When you are helping someone, the helping is always appropriate to the circumstances. Sometimes that means kicking the crutch out from under someone and letting him fall, taking the crutch away and hiding it, forcing him to get up on his own two feet and walk. You encourage, goad, pull, but always the other person must do the work. You can only help others help themselves with their pain and struggle. At the same time,

IN A SENSE, COMPASSION IS THE ACT OF BEING SELFISH.

you do what is appropriate. You act according to imperative, not with sentimentality or romance, but according to
the circumstances. This only works when there's no separation between the doer, the act of doing, and the thing or
person being done to. They become one reality, one act.
Shinko had to reach out! He had to reach out desperately,
otherwise there would have been no teaching. It couldn't
have happened until he raised the bodhi mind, the mind
of enlightenment.

Where there's no entry barrier, we cannot help but
waste the potential of an otherwise fine student. The barrier strengthens those who will accomplish, and it discour-
ages those who are not ready, or who should be using
another process. This is a very important point. Knowing
the nature of the self, the nature of reality, realizing it for
oneself rather than understanding it or believing it, is
where compassion arises. Once one has been transformed
by the realization, that realization in activity manifests itself as compassion. When a teacher pulls the rug out from
under a student and the student falls, that pulling the rug
out is called "holding back." That's what Bodhidharma was
doing, holding back, letting the student reach. When the
student falls, the teacher rushes over, helps him up, gets
him on his feet, makes sure he's steady, and then pulls the
rug out again. Down he goes. The teacher rushes over,
picks him up, pulls the rug out again. Down he goes. The
teacher rushes over . . . and the process is repeated again
and again until the time when the rug comes out and the
student does not fall. Then the student is no longer a
student; the teacher is no longer a teacher. This is the
merging of teacher and student, in which parent becomes
child and child becomes parent.

Acting in accord with the imperative: "My mind is not
yet at peace. I beg you, my teacher, please give it peace."
Shinko was pushed down into the abyss of despair by the
demand of Bodhidharma, "Bring it here!" He was driven
right to the wall. His reasoning was of no help. He wasn't

THE TEACH-
ER PULLS
THE RUG
OUT FROM
UNDER THE
STUDENT.

20

aware of whether he was alive or dead. He couldn't even utter a moaning cry. "Bring the mind to me and I'll set it at rest." "I have searched for the mind and it is finally unobtainable." We should appreciate the weeks, the months, even years between Bodhidharma's demand, "Bring your mind to me and I'll set it at rest," and Shinko's answer, "I have searched for the mind and it is finally unobtainable." Master Rinzai, who was described as "a monk of pure, single-hearted discipline," once spoke of the time before his enlightenment: "I was in sheer darkness altogether." Hakuin said, "I felt as if I were sitting in an ice cave ten thousand miles thick. I myself shall never forget the spiritual struggle I had in sheer darkness for years."

In Catholicism this despair is called "the dark night of the soul." In Zen we call it "descending into the cave of the blue dragon." There are no shortcuts. You'll see the advertising promising *satori* in one weekend. That's just bullshit, and most of us know it. We've got an entire lifetime of conditioning to work through, and that doesn't happen in a weekend. Enlightenment itself is a moment, but before the moment arrives, the pump needs to be primed by single-minded practice. That is why it is so important to have the proper state of mind before entering training. Anything less than that would be deceiving. It would be saying to you that you can't do it, when you *can* do it! Every one of us can do it. Each one of us has all the equipment to do it. We are all fully equipped Buddhas. But if the aspiration doesn't exist, if the mind of the student doesn't exist, it is hopeless. It won't happen, and to imply otherwise would be dishonest. So we create the barrier gate to test the perseverance of the student. In a traditional monastery, the monk who is the guardian of the gate chases people away: "Go away. We don't want you here."

The monk persists, "Please, I must come. I must study."

"Go away. We don't have any room. The Master doesn't want any more students."

The monk simply persists, sometimes for days. If he gets

"I SHALL NEVER FORGET THE SPIRITUAL STRUGGLE I HAD IN SHEER DARKNESS FOR YEARS."

WE ARE ALL FULLY EQUIPPED BUDDHAS.

by the gatekeeper to the entrance of the main monastery, he must sit on the steps and wait to be acknowledged, and that will only come if great determination born of a deep spiritual quest is evident. This tradition of the barrier of the gate has continued for thousands of years.

Someone once asked me, "Does Zen do the same thing psychotherapy does?" In a sense, yes; and in a sense, no. Zen is concerned with spiritual life. It is not concerned with adjusting to your relationship or to your job, although such adjustment is a by-product of Zen because once you understand and realize fully the ground of being, that understanding penetrates into all aspects of existence. But if what you are looking for is to be well adjusted, then you should be doing therapy. If you're concerned with physical well-being, a health spa is a good place to go. In spite of the fact that physical and mental well-being are part of our practice, our aspiration goes beyond that. We need to concern ourselves with the ground of being, the ultimate nature of reality. Otherwise, we are wasting our time.

OUR ASPIRA-
TION GOES
BEYOND THE
DESIRE FOR
WELL-BEING.

Everyone is already enlightened—so what need is there to practice? No question about it, each one of us already has the Buddha nature. No question about it, each one of us, just as we are, is perfect and complete. There is nothing to attain, and yet we struggle! Why? Because we believe that each one of us is perfect and complete. Because we understand that each one of us is perfect and complete. And because we haven't *realized* that each one of us is perfect and complete. When we realize it, we make ourselves free. When we believe it, we make ourselves prisoners of that belief. When we understand it, we make a cage out of understanding—we bind ourselves. Only the realization, the direct, intimate, personal experience of it is transformative; only that can make you free. Everything else—believing, understanding—is the words, the ideas that describe reality, not the reality itself. This is the proper transmission of this dharma. Anything else is just an imitation, not the real thing.

ONLY
DIRECT
PERSONAL
EXPERIENCE
CAN MAKE
YOU FREE.

22

"It" can be found on this mountain,
But its exact whereabouts is unknown.
The way is difficult and steep,
Strewn with boulders, shrouded in mist.
Only a few will reach the peak

All it takes is the determination to do it. You have everything else you need. Just decide to do it. Not tomorrow—tomorrow always remains tomorrow. Do it now. DO IT NOW. Commit yourself now. Once you have committed yourself to doing it, it is done. The rest is only a matter of time.

3

An Introduction to Zazen

IN ZAZEN we begin by working with the breath as a means of bringing our scattered energy into focus and quieting thoughts that continually arise. If we practice faithfully, the power of concentration develops little by little, and eventually this discipline enables us to penetrate, awaken, and know our true self.

First we choose an appropriate place to sit. It should be a quiet and private space, preferably one that will be used only for zazen. It should be neat, attractive, and free from clutter and visual distractions. Incense helps to provide a tranquil atmosphere and a sense of form, particularly when one sits alone. A stick of incense can be used to time the sitting period—a short stick for half an hour, a long one for forty-five minutes. You will need a mat or a large, flat cushion, and a small thick cushion (or cushions) to raise you about four or five inches off the ground. Or you may sit on a firm, straight-backed chair. You will need to wear loose, comfortable clothing so that circulation is not restricted. For most people, the best times for zazen are the early morning and the evening, when there are fewer interruptions and when physical and mental energies are less scattered.

There are a number of different positions that are used in zazen: full lotus, half lotus, cross-legged, *seiza* (sitting on a cushion over the heels with the knees straight ahead), and several other variations. Experiment until you find

THIS DISCI-
PLINE ENA-
BLES US TO
PENETRATE,
AWAKEN,
AND KNOW
OUR TRUE
SELF.

25

one that is comfortable and stable. The actual position you choose is not as important as your posture. If you are using a cushion, your knees should be resting on the mat so that you have a stable base, and you should be well balanced, with your pelvis tilted slightly forward, so that you can sit upright without tension in your back, shoulders, or legs. If your posture is correct, your spine will hold you up with virtually no strain. You may need, especially at first, an extra cushion or prop to achieve this balance. (The same is true for sitting on a chair.) Once you are sitting straight, blood vessels, nerves, and organs will be able to function freely. This posture allows your diaphragm to expand without restriction, so that breathing is natural, even, and relaxed.

Begin by first rocking in gentle arcs from side to side, gradually diminishing them until you feel centered. Then stretch forward with a straight back and slowly straighten up. These movements will help you find your center of gravity in the lower abdomen, about two inches below the navel. Your neck should be straight and your chin level. Push the top of your head toward the ceiling, and feel as if you are stretching your whole spine. Settle down slowly, keeping your spine straight. No part of the body should be stiff or rigid. Let your eyes close halfway and direct your gaze about three feet in front of your knees. Do not stare, but let the eyes go out of focus. Your hands should rest close to your abdomen, palms up, left on top of right, with thumbs lightly touching. The tongue sits against the roof of the mouth, behind the front teeth. Breathe through your nose, keeping your teeth and lips gently closed. Swallow once—this creates a mild suction in the mouth and seems to prevent constant salivation and swallowing. Let go of all tension in your body.

Breathing and posture are closely allied to emotions. And you will notice, as thoughts arise, how thought and emotion are connected. Thoughts may produce anger, anxiety, resentment, and so on, and these emotions in turn

NO PART OF THE BODY SHOULD BE STIFF OR RIGID.

YOU WILL NOTICE, AS THOUGHTS ARISE, HOW THOUGHT AND EMOTION ARE CONNECTED.

affect the depth and rate of breathing and produce tensions—subtle or obvious—throughout the body. Learn to feel the tensions in your body. Is your jaw clenched? Are your shoulders hunched, diaphragm and abdomen rigid? In sitting and in daily life, try to return to an open, balanced posture and full, even breathing. As you recognize and consciously work with your body and breath patterns during meditation and all your daily activities, you gradually uncover a calmer, more stable emotional state.

LEARN TO FEEL THE TENSIONS IN YOUR BODY.

Once you've settled down, let your abdominal muscles relax as much as possible. When you've been doing zazen for a while, the lower belly will begin to work like a bellows, as if filling and emptying with each breath. It is not a matter of pushing and contracting the stomach; the volume of air moves it—we learn to breathe the way a young infant does. Many people habitually breathe with the chest, or with tension in the stomach or abdomen. As we do zazen we learn to let the breath sink into the abdomen. Breathing becomes very deep and even. Be aware of your breath and of any feeling in the lower abdomen. Sooner or later you will feel the breath moving the lower belly. Do not overfill your lungs or empty them to the point of strain, or hold your breath. Once your breathing is regular and very comfortable, you can extend the out-breath gently or simply wait until the inhalation begins by itself, and next time wait a little longer. As the out-breath slows, you will ground yourself more deeply in your center. The inhalation should be effortless. Just let go—let your lungs fill naturally.

JUST LET GO—LET YOUR LUNGS FILL NATURALLY.

When your body is relaxed and your breath is stable, you are ready to begin the basic technique that we use in zazen for developing concentration: counting the breath. As you begin to exhale, count that exhalation as number one. Count your inhalation as two, your next exhalation as three, and so on until you reach ten. Then start again, on the next breath, with "one," and repeat the counting from one to ten, over and over. When thoughts appear and you are distracted by them and begin chasing them, return to number one and start over. This is very important. You make this basic agreement with yourself: to begin again each time you find that your attention is not really on the breath. Random thoughts will come and go—that is inevitable. But when you chase them, when, for example, you remember you should have mailed a certain letter yesterday—say, the payment of your electric bill, and then you start to think, what will happen if the check does not get there before the fifteenth? and will they turn off the electricity? and will you be able to get an extension?—then you are involved in a whole mental process, a train of thought. You may still be counting your breath (if so, you are probably up to a hundred and fifty), but your attention is definitely not on it. Remembering the overdue bill, by itself, is not chasing thoughts. Thoughts of all kinds will arise. When a thought arises, we learn to observe it and let it disappear. Then we gently return the attention to counting the breath. Do not try to suppress thoughts. Observe them, witness them, and then, without judging, redirect your attention to your breath.

WHEN A THOUGHT ARISES, OB- SERVE IT AND LET IT DISAPPEAR.

For most of us, many weeks or months may go by before we can reach the count of ten for the first time without distracting thoughts. What we are doing in observing and counting the breath is developing the power of concentration. Gradually concentration can be focused for longer and longer periods of time. But it is important to be patient and not expect instant results. Learning this skill and slowly deepening the power of concentration may take months or even years. It is also important to sit regularly. Try to make an agreement with yourself to sit each day at a particular time for a certain amount of time—ten to fifteen minutes is sufficient in the beginning. It is more effective to sit consistently fifteen minutes a day than it is to sit for two or three hours every now and then.

Once the counting of the breath has been learned and concentration, true one-pointedness of mind, has developed, we usually go on to other practices, such as following the breath, koan study, or *shikantaza* ("just sitting"—formless zazen). But we should not think of these in terms of "gain" or "promotion." And we should not think of counting the breath as just a preparation for the real thing. It is the real thing. Whatever our practice is, we put ourselves into it completely. When counting the breath, we just count the breath.

It is important to be patient and persistent, not thinking of a goal, not thinking of how the sitting practice may help us. We just put ourselves into it and let go of our thoughts, opinions, positions, everything our minds hold on to. The human mind is basically free, not clinging. In zazen we learn to uncover that mind, to see who we really are.

THE HUMAN MIND IS BASICALLY FREE, NOT CLINGING.

4

A TALK ON THE HEART SUTRA

AVALOKITESHVARA BODHISATTVA,
doing deep prajna paramita,
Clearly saw emptiness of all the five conditions,
Thus completely relieving misfortune and pain.
O Shariputra, form is no other than emptiness,
    Emptiness no other than form;
    Form is exactly emptiness, emptiness exactly form.
Sensation, conception, discrimination, awareness
    Are likewise like this.
O Shariputra, all dharmas are forms of emptiness,
    Not born, not destroyed,
    Not stained, not pure,
    Without loss, without gain.
So, in emptiness there is no form,
    No sensation, conception, discrimination,
        awareness,
    No eye, ear, nose, tongue, body, mind,
    No color, sound, smell, taste, touch, phenomena,
    No realm of sight, no realm of consciousness,
    No ignorance and no end to ignorance,
    No old age and death, and no end to old age
        and death,
    No suffering, no cause of suffering,
        no extinguishing,
        no path,

No wisdom and no gain.
No gain, and thus the bodhisattva lives prajna
   paramita
With no hindrance in the mind
No hindrance, therefore no fear.
Far beyond deluded thoughts, this is nirvana.
All past, present, and future Buddhas
      live prajna paramita
   And therefore attain anuttara-samyak-sambodhi.
Therefore, know prajna paramita is the great mantra,
   The vivid mantra, the best mantra,
   The unsurpassable mantra.
It completely clears all pain—this is the truth,
      not a lie.
So set forth the prajna paramita mantra.
Set forth this mantra and say:

    Gate! Gate! Paragate! Parasamgate!
    Bodhi svaha! Prajna Heart Sutra!

THIS SUTRA IS THE FOUNDATION OF THE BUDDHA'S TEACHING.

In the sutras, the words of the Buddha and some of the greatest ancient masters are recorded and handed down. They are usually in the form of a talk or a dialogue directed to a disciple. In *The Heart Sutra*, Avalokiteshvara is speaking to Shariputra. This small sutra, which is a condensation of the much longer *Perfection of Wisdom Sutra*, is a very important teaching. In fact, it is said to be the foundation of the teaching of the Buddha.

The first thing we should look at is the title. In the translation of the title we use, *Maha Prajna Paramita Heart Sutra*, we've retained Sanskrit terms that are not really translatable. There are rough English equivalents, but they don't carry the same connotation, so the meaning is somewhat different. The word *maha* literally means "great," but more than that it means "boundless," without edges, without end. At the same time it means "great" in the sense of "all-pervading." *Prajna* we can translate as "wisdom," but this is misleading. In the West we equate wisdom with *knowing*, although implicit in the idea of knowledge is separation between the knower and the thing known. You must have a knower to have knowledge. The basis of prajna is the realization of no separation: no knower, no knowing, nothing to be known. Although we very loosely translate *prajna* as "wisdom," keep in mind that they are not the same thing. *Paramita* literally means "the other shore," the shore of enlightenment. There are six paramitas, six practices that naturally express the enlightened mind. Prajna paramita, the practice of "wisdom," contains and includes all the others. Maha Prajna Paramita is "the great wisdom of the other shore." *Heart Sutra* in Japanese is *Shingyo*. We translate *shin* as "heart" or "mind." It is the Chinese character for feeling and emotion, but also for mind. Chinese characters typically have this kind of depth, pointing to more than one way of seeing something.

NO KNOWER, NO KNOWING, NOTHING TO BE KNOWN.

The sutra begins: *Avalokiteshvara Bodhisattva, doing deep prajna paramita* . . . Avalokiteshvara is one of the traditional bodhisattvas of India, the Bodhisattva of Compassion, the hearer of the cries of the world. Usually depicted as a woman or as an androgynous figure, this bodhisattva is looked on by Buddhists of many different sects as the embodiment of compassion. In the West, compassion is usually associated with the idea of "doing good," being a helper or a savior. We should look, however, at what compassion really is. The best way of seeing how it functions is to look again at what wisdom, prajna, is. The best example I know is one that Yasutani Roshi was fond of using. Suppose I were to take "I-consciousness," ego-consciousness, and give that to my two hands, so that each hand has the sense that it is separate and distinct from everything else. This is our most basic premise, that the skin bag that contains us is separate and distinct; this is the way we live our life. Suppose each of these hands is an "I." If someone puts money in the right hand, the left hand becomes angry: "Why do you give money to the right hand? How come the left hand never gets any?" If the right hand gets caught in a fire, the left hand would love to help it. But being a separate hand, it would have to take a big chance to reach into the fire and help the right hand. Maybe it would do it, but there would definitely be hesitation. After all, it is a question of survival. If you enlighten the two hands, suddenly they realize that they are two parts of the same reality, yourself, and that there is no separation between the two. If you put money in the left hand, the right hand has it. If the left hand gets caught in a fire, the right hand responds to the pain. No question, no hesitation, no separation. That realization of no separation is wisdom: prajna. The right hand saving the left is a selfish act, because in true compassion the person you help is not separate from yourself; you are both part of the same reality. This compassion, arising from prajna, functions the way you grow your hair—without effort, without the intention of "doing good."

THE REALI-
ZATION OF
NO SEPARA-
TION IS
WISDOM.

Avalokiteshvara Bodhisattva, deeply realizing the wisdom of the other shore, "clearly saw emptiness of all the five conditions." The five conditions are what we call the skandhas in Buddhism. *Skandha* in Sanskrit is an "aggregate" or "collection." The first skandha is form, material substance; the second is sensation, feeling; the third is thought, conception, or sense perception; the fourth is discrimination; and the fifth is consciousness, which ties all five together. The five skandhas are the modes of being that form our view of reality.

Avalokiteshvara Bodhisattva, doing deep prajna paramita, clearly saw emptiness of all the five conditions, thus completely relieving misfortune and pain. The five skandhas viewed with the awakened eye are seen to be fundamentally empty of all characteristics: pure, unstained, untarnishable. If the skandhas are viewed through ignorance (delusion), we create the false notion of a self. We think that the self is everything inside this bag of skin and that everything outside of it is the rest of the universe. This is how we create pain. The moment we hold the thought of a separate self, thirst and desire and all the dualities—heaven and hell, gain and loss, good and bad—come into being. When we realize that we are everything, what can we possibly want? What is there to lose or gain?

Next Avalokiteshvara says: *O Shariputra, form is no other than emptiness, emptiness no other than form.* Form is the five conditions, and emptiness is the absence of form. But Avalokiteshvara is telling Shariputra, over and over, that form and emptiness are the same thing. *O Shariputra, form is no other than emptiness; emptiness no other than form; form is exactly emptiness, emptiness exactly form.* In English, "emptiness," or "the Great Void," sounds like a vacancy, a big black hole. It is not. It is full, filled with everything. Avalokiteshvara goes on: *Sensation, conception, discrimination, awareness are likewise like this.* He is saying it again—the skandhas are empty. What we see, perceive, hear, feel, and think is all empty. The ten thousand dharmas, all the phenomena in the universe, are empty. The self is empty.

O Shariputra, all dharmas are forms of emptiness, not born, not destroyed. How could *it* be born? How could *it* end? Where does *it* come from to be born? *It* contains everything. You and I contain everything. When we really see that, we realize what is meant by the Buddhist teaching that birth is the unborn and death the unextinguished. What is it that is born? What is it that dies? This is not philosophy. This sutra states the direct experience of Shakyamuni Buddha and the thousands of Buddhas that came afterward, the men and women who have come to realization over the past 2,500 years.

YOU AND I CONTAIN EVERY-THING.

O Shariputra, all dharmas are forms of emptiness, not born, not destroyed, not stained, not pure, without loss, without gain. So in emptiness there is no form, no sensation, conception, discrimination, awareness. No eye, ear, nose, tongue, body, mind. No color, sound, smell, taste, touch, phenomena. No realm of sight, no realm of consciousness. Yet that emptiness is, in fact, form. When we forget the self, there is nothing in the universe other than our self: nothing to compare, name, or identify. When it is the only thing there is, how can we talk about it?

How can we see it? We cannot help but *be* it—the tree, the sound of the river, the sunrise, a baby's cry, through and through. That is a whole different dimension of reality.

The sutra goes on: *No ignorance and no end to ignorance. No old age and death, and no end to old age and death. No suffering, no cause of suffering, no extinguishing, no path, no wisdom and no gain. No gain, and thus the bodhisattva lives prajna paramita.* Both sides, form and emptiness, are being shown. You and I are the same: *emptiness.* Yet I am not you and you are not me: *form.* This is very difficult to grasp intellectually. The left hemisphere of the brain works in a linear and sequential manner; we grasp things dualistically, relatively. Our conception of the universe is relative: everything is known and defined in reference to something else. When I used to work as a scientist, I realized that science was all one big reference system. You go from one reference point to another. How do you get back beyond that? What is the root, the absolute basis of the whole thing?

It is important to see that emptiness. When we do, it transforms our way of seeing reality, of living our life. It doesn't mean abandoning the relative. Obviously, the relative is necessary. I can't get across the street unless I know the difference between the street, the car, and myself. To function in the world we must understand the relative, but at the same time we should see the emptiness that underlies it all. It makes a big difference in how we function and the degree of bondage we place upon ourselves. *No wisdom and no gain.* If you realize that you are the whole thing, that there is nothing outside of yourself, that you are as vast and boundless as the universe itself, that everything is empty of self-nature, then there is no way to gain: you already contain everything. There is no way to lose anything. Where could it go?

EVERY-
THING IS
EMPTY OF
SELF-
NATURE.

Thus the bodhisattva lives prajna paramita, with no hindrance in the mind. No hindrance, therefore no fear. Hindrance comes from our own mind. What are the limits, the boundaries?

We place them on ourselves. With no hindrance in the mind, there is no fear, nothing to lose, nothing to hold on to. *Far beyond deluded thoughts, this is nirvana.* This very moment is nirvana; this very body is the body of the Buddha, the Enlightened One. This very mind is the mind of the Buddha. *All past, present, and future Buddhas live prajna paramita.* The wisdom of the other shore is the very life of the Buddha. *All past, present, and future Buddhas live prajna paramita and therefore attain anuttara-samyak-sambodhi.* This is a Sanskrit phrase that we translate as "supreme perfect enlightenment." *Enlightenment* is really just a stinky word that Zen teachers use. Form is emptiness and emptiness is form. Just to hold a thought that there is a distinction between Buddhas, enlightened ones, and ordinary beings is the worst kind of delusion. There are many koans that use that trap to snare people who are hooked by enlightenment. The reason the word is ridiculous is that there is nothing to attain. If you've opened your mind's eye and realized yourself and think that you've attained something, you have gotten nowhere.

"*Therefore, know that prajna paramita is the great mantra, the vivid mantra, the best mantra, the unsurpassable mantra. It completely clears all pain—this is the truth, not a lie.* A mantra is the chant of the soul. Chanting with the whole body and mind, we become totally intimate with the mantra and totally realize this *Maha Prajna Paramita Heart Sutra.* When it is your life, when your activity and the activity of the Buddha are the same activity, then you've liberated yourself. That is being the mantra. In order to do that, you have to forget the self, to let go of that idea that separates you from everything else in the universe.

The whole sutra can be reduced to *Maha Prajna Paramita Heart Sutra.* That says the whole thing, contains all the volumes of teachings. It could even be reduced to just *Maha.* To really be Maha is to forget the self; to forget the self is to be as vast and as boundless as the universe. To be Maha, to penetrate it completely, is to see this sutra for

THIS VERY MOMENT IS NIRVANA; THIS VERY BODY IS THE BODY OF THE BUDDHA.

IT IS TO BE
REALIZED,
NOT BE-
LIEVED, UN-
DERSTOOD,
OR
ANALYZED.

yourself, not as a bunch of words being chanted, but as a manifestation of your life. Unless each one of us personally experiences this, it doesn't mean anything. It is to be *realized*, not believed, understood, or analyzed, but directly, immediately realized with your own life. When you do that, you make yourself free! You become and manifest the Buddha.

So set forth the prajna paramita mantra. Set forth this mantra and say: "Gate! Gate! Paragate! Parasamgate! Bodhi svaha! Prajna Heart Sutra." We loosely translate this, "Go, go, hurry quickly, go to the other shore. Cross over, cross over to the other side, the other shore of enlightenment." We should realize that the other shore and this shore are the same shore, the same thing. When you've realized that, not just believed or accepted it, you've crossed over. The transmission is complete; your mind and the mind of the Buddha are one. But whether you realize it or not, your mind and the mind of the Buddha are one. Anything that could be said about this wonderful sutra would miss it, because the truth does not lie in the words but in the reality itself.

5

Are You Awake?

WHAT IS "taking responsibility for our lives"? We usually think of taking responsibility in the sense of meeting our commitments and obligations, keeping our word, paying our bills, taking care of things—our business, family, home, health. But there is another way of looking at responsibility. "Taking responsibility for my life" literally means that I am responsible for my life, for who and what I am, for what happens to me. I am responsible for what my experience is and how I experience it.

But how can we be responsible for all of this when we are constantly tossed to and fro by circumstances? This happens not only to us, but to everybody around us. We have a disappointment, a setback, an accident, an argument, a loss, we do not get what we want or we do get what we want. Or the cause is more mysterious—it is something to do with the stars, or our biorhythms, or the vibes in this place, or that we didn't eat right or get enough sleep. However you cut it, you find yourself one day wishing you were dead, and two days later happy to be alive, ten feet off the ground—and maybe the circumstances are the same. Sooner or later you are tossed back in the other direction. How can we be responsible when we are not free, when we are bound and restricted in this way, living at the mercy of circumstances?

In a famous koan from Mumon's *Gateless Gate,* Master Zuigan talks about being master of one's life:

"TAKING RESPONSI-BILITY FOR MY LIFE" MEANS THAT I AM RE-SPONSIBLE FOR WHAT HAPPENS TO ME.

41

> Every day Master Zuigan used to call out to himself,
> "Oh, Master!"
> And he would answer himself, "Yes?"
> "Are you awake?" he would ask.
> And he would answer, "Yes, I am,"
> "Never be deceived by others—any day, any time."
> "No, I will not."

That question, "Are you awake?," is the same as "Are you enlightened? Are you aware of your life?" The word *others* refers to circumstances. If you are not "deceived by others," you are not tossed back and forth by conditions. You are in charge of your life. Of course, it is not really the conditions that toss us back and forth; it is our conditioning, which is based on our particular circumstances— where and how we grew up, what school we went to, who our parents were, what we learned from friends, books, TV. We find ourselves living out that conditioning, that programming, for the rest of our lives. Most of us are conditioned in very much the same way, which makes it easier to live together in society, to get things done, to understand the rules. Our conditioning is what makes advertising so successful, making it possible for people in the advertising industry to get us to respond to their products the way they want us to. The whole point of advertising is to create a need where none exists; that is, to stimulate desire. Desire is fundamental—a basic underlying force in our life. Once we desire something, we can be led around by the nose.

DESIRE ARISES FROM THE BELIEF THAT SOMETHING IS LACKING.

Desire arises from the belief that something is lacking, that somehow we need something we do not have, that we are incomplete. The origin of desire is in the discriminating consciousness that makes us distinguish "this" from "that," "self" from "other." That separation of self from other is based on ignorance, on not knowing what is real, and it creates all our suffering. When there is self, there is other, there is gain and loss, something we want to get, something or someone we can not bear to lose. That is how

we create greed, anger, confusion, despair. When we believe that our "self" is whatever is inside this bag of skin, we
feel incomplete, cut off from everything else in the universe, and our desire is really the desire to make whatever
we feel we lack a part of ourself. Underneath our particular desire is the desire to heal the split, to become one with
what we think is "out there." When you realize that there is
nothing outside of you, then there is no way of being incomplete, nothing to desire, nothing that is not you. Without the illusion of a separate self, there is no gain and no
loss.

I can tell you that the self is an idea, that it does not exist.
You can even believe it, but that isn't going to change
anything. You will still respond to circumstances according
to your programming. Even if it makes sense to you and
you can justify it logically, you will still respond from the
basis of a separate self because of conditioning. When you
realize firsthand, by going very deep into yourself, that the
self is empty, only then does the beginning of emancipa
tion occur. Even then, the programming continues like a
reflex action. But once you've realized that the self is empty, the reflex loses all its power. You don't have to do
anything about it; all you need to do is to be aware, to
continue the same practice you've been doing from the
beginning. When angry, you acknowledge that you are
angry and let it go. Each time, your anger will get a little
weaker. The same thing is true if you haven't yet realized
yourself. With great faith you acknowledge the feeling
each time it comes up, and let it go.

Being awake is taking responsibility for your life, knowing that circumstances are just yourself—that what you do
and what happens to you are the same thing. The consequences and the experience of your life result from the
activities of your life. These activities are what you do,
what you say, and what you think. We create karma with
our thoughts just as much as with our actions. When you
take responsibility, you are not tossed around by circum-

WITHOUT THE ILLU-SION OF A SEPARATE SELF, THERE IS NO GAIN AND NO LOSS.

stances; there is no one to blame and no one to be a victim. You can't blame it on the President, because the President is nothing but yourself. You can't blame it on the Russians; they are nothing but yourself. You begin to see the world and what is happening around you in a very different way.

When you realize that the self is complete, that it contains everything and isn't separate from "the ten thousand things," emancipation begins. Gradually, instead of greed, anger, and ignorance, there is compassion, wisdom, and enlightenment. The greed, instead of serving a separate self, begins to serve all beings. When you know that the guy lying in the street bleeding is you, you greedily take care of yourself. You pick him up and comfort him, with no sense of separation and no sense of doing "good." And when you realize that this earth, this environment, is your very life, there is no way to foul it. Compassion, wisdom, and enlightenment are the activity of no-self.

COMPASSION, WISDOM, AND ENLIGHTENMENT ARE THE ACTIVITY OF NO-SELF.

Zuigan tells us that it is time to take responsibility and be the masters of our lives, to get to the ground of being and realize who we are, to penetrate the nature of reality and learn to live our lives out of what we realize. This unnamable reality that Zuigan calls "Master" is the same as Master Eno's "original face," and Master Rinzai's "true person of no rank." Zen masters are compelled to speak, to find a way to point to this one reality. The aim of Zen practice is the direct experience of each of us in opening our spiritual eye to the absolute subjectivity of coming to be ourselves. One has to give one's body and mind to it. Mumon emphasized this when he set up the first koan in *The Gateless Gate*. He said that "one must pass the barriers set by the ancient Zen masters. For the attainment of incomparable satori, one has to cast away the discriminating mind."

We seem to know a great deal about the rest of the universe and very little about ourselves. That is what the study of Buddhism is—a way to find out about ourselves. Buckminster Fuller once tried to make an "Operating Manual for the Spaceship Earth." Well, the operating manual for human existence cannot be written—it is transmitted from mind to mind. Nobody can do it for you, and nobody can tell you about it. You have to find out for yourself—you have to realize it directly. When we free ourselves from the delusion that we are only what is inside this bag of skin, we realize that we are as vast and complete as the universe itself. Just like the water bird—the great blue heron—that comes here to Basho Pond:

> It comes and it goes
> Leaving no traces at all
> Yet knows how to go its own way.

IT IS TRANSMITTED FROM MIND TO MIND.

It is completely the master. Shouldn't our lives be as clear as the life of that great blue heron? As the life of the fly that is buzzing here now? As the sun that rises in the east and sets in the west? Somehow we lose our way; everything gets in a muddle. It doesn't need to be that way. The Third Noble Truth of the Buddha is that it is possible to put an end to pain, to free ourselves from the karma of birth and death, to be master of our own life. Who is this "Master"? Each one of us must find out for ourselves. We should go deeply into ourselves and experience the ground of our being and learn to live our lives out of this realization. This life is too precious to waste.

THIS LIFE IS TOO PRECIOUS TO WASTE.

6

Ceaseless Practice

Based on Master Dogen's
Shobogenzo: "Ceaseless Practice"

SINCE practice and the Way are neither large nor small, neither self nor other, neither existing previously nor just arising now, they therefore exist "thus." Cause and effect is ceaseless practice; however, ceaseless practice is not cause and effect. We should see this clearly. The ceaseless practice which manifests ceaseless practice is none other than the ceaseless practice of this very moment.

MAIN CASE

The Great Master Dogen taught, "In the great way of the Buddhas and ancestors, surely there is a supreme ceaseless practice which continues endlessly. There is not the slightest gap between awakening the mind, practice, enlightenment, and nirvana. Ceaseless practice continually revolves. Therefore, it does not depend on individual powerful acts nor on the spirit of others. It is undefiled, ceaseless practice. The virtue of ceaseless practice maintains self and others. Essentially, our ceaseless practice fills heaven and earth, and influences everything with its virtue. Although we may be unaware of it, it still occurs.

VERSE

Vast and boundless, nothing is hidden
In clear water, all the way to the bottom
The fish swims like a fish.
Vast limitless sky, transparent throughout
The bird flies like a bird.
Extremely subtle and profound—
How can I explain?

We say that to really practice the breath means to be the breath with the whole body and mind. To really practice *Mu* means to be Mu with the whole body and mind, day and night: Mu sits, Mu walks, Mu rests. To see the koan is to be the koan. What does it mean to practice Mu twenty-four hours a day, every day? The interesting thing is that whether we practice Mu twenty-four hours a day or not, Mu practices twenty-four hours a day, every day. The key to seeing it is to close the gap that separates ourselves from it. Ceaseless practice is not some kind of theoretical, philosophical, or esoteric idea. It is the ceaseless practice that has continued for 2,500 years.

Ceaseless practice immediately contains raising the bodhi mind, practice, enlightenment, and nirvana of not only oneself, but of all Buddhas of the past, present, and future. Dogen teaches that the merit of the ceaseless practice of Buddhas and ancestors has the ability to "save humans and gods"—to save not only all sentient beings, but all deities as well—all things in heaven and hell.

This is the manifestation of the hands and eyes of great compassion. In order to save a god, you must be god; only a god can save a god. In order to save humans, you must be human. In order to receive the Buddha's transmission, you must be a Buddha to begin with. Buddhas can only transmit to Buddhas. Each act of compassion is the life of the Buddhas and ancestors. Each act of compassion manifests the virtue of ceaseless practice. However, gods and humans don't know that they are being helped by the

EACH ACT OF COMPASSION MANIFESTS THE VIRTUE OF CEASELESS PRACTICE.

ceaseless practice of Buddhas and ancestors. Why don't they know it?

The ultimate truth is boundless. It is vast; there is no edge to it. How can we speak of it in terms of knowing or not knowing? Knowing is being caught up in the words and the ideas that describe it. Not knowing is blank consciousness. The ultimate truth that pervades everywhere can't be grasped by knowing or not knowing. How will we realize it? When we have correctly transmitted the truth to ourselves, at that very moment, we manifest the truth.

THE ULTI-MATE TRUTH CAN'T BE GRASPED BY KNOWING OR NOT KNOWING.

Master Dogen writes:

> From the ceaseless practice of all Buddhas and ancestors, our own ceaseless practice emerges and we can attain the Way. From our own ceaseless practice, the ceaseless practice of all Buddhas emerges and the Buddhas attain the Great Way. From our own ceaseless practice there is endless virtue; accordingly, all the Buddhas and ancestors endlessly live as Buddha, transcend Buddha, have the mind of Buddha, and become Buddha. Through ceaseless practice sun, moon, and stars move, the great earth and vast space, the right body and mind and the four great elements and five skandhas exist. Ceaseless practice is not in the places where people seek, yet all must return to it. Through the ceaseless practice of all Buddhas of past, present, and future, all the Buddhas of the past, present, and future emerge. The virtue of ceaseless practice is never hidden, therefore the mind is aroused and practice begins. Its virtue, however, is not immediately revealed and thus it cannot be seen, heard, or comprehended. Although it is not revealed, do not study it as something hidden.

Dogen has such an amazing way of teaching. I think clearly he is the greatest of the ancient masters. His dharma is completely interwoven with the reality of everyday existence. We have to understand that for him, everyday existence was his life as a monk at a monastery, but the very same things that apply to the monastery can apply to any place else in the world. Many of the same things have to get accomplished in the world as in the monastery—you need to prepare food, wash yourself, clean the place, sow the garden. In our case, daily life is even more similar to the practice of lay practitioners than one might think. We at Zen Mountain Monastery are very much like the "outside": the computer needs to be operated, the bills need to be paid, our journal needs to be published, and so on. What Dogen did was to make monastic rules on how to wash your face, how to use the lavatory, how to cook—he covered virtually everything involved in taking care of one's personal self as well as in taking care of the monastery and the dharma. His master work, the *Shobogenzo* (Treasury of the True Dharma Eye), is a collection of these "rules," and it is the most profound and subtle teaching of the Buddhadharma ever revealed. His very practical instructions are presented always from the point of view of the realization of the interpenetration of all things, of the mutual nonhindrance of all things.

"In the great way of Buddhas and ancestors there is supreme ceaseless practice that continues endlessly. There is not the slightest gap between awakening the mind, practice, enlightenment and nirvana." These opening sentences contain, in a way, the whole of this chapter by Dogen.

"AWAKEN-ING THE MIND" IS RAISING THE BODHI MIND. "Awakening the mind" is the raising of the bodhi mind. To raise the bodhi mind means to raise the mind that aspires to enlightenment. The bodhi mind *is* the mind of enlightenment. The moment the bodhi mind is raised, all of the realization and actualization of Buddhas of the past, present, and future are manifested. In the ten stages of our training at Doshinji, the first stage is "the search for the way," and it means to realize that there is a possibility to put an end to suffering. It is to realize that something is not quite right, that life is suffering—the same realization of the Buddha—and that this suffering is not necessary, that it is possible to put an end to it. To raise the bodhi mind is the wisdom of the Four Noble Truths: life is suffering, the cause of suffering, the cessation of suffering, and how to put an end to suffering. Raising the bodhi mind is the realization of not only the Buddha, but the thousands of Buddhas that succeed him, not only up to the present, but into the future.

It sounds very mystical, and it is. It is as mystical as a bird taking wing. Think for a minute of one of those birds that you can buy in a department store, a canary raised for the purpose of being sold. From the time it is in the egg until you receive it, it has been in a cage. All that it knows is the confines of that cage. When suddenly one day the cage door is opened and the bird stands on the edge, it will leap intuitively into space. It doesn't know about flying; there is not much flying that can go on in the confines of a cage. But immediately this bird that has never flown knows how to fly, and the minute it leaps into the air and takes wing, it manifests the truth of all birds of the past, present, and future.

IT IS AS MYSTICAL AS A BIRD TAKING WING.

I remember when my son was young, he received a gift of a little turtle that had "Florida" or something written on its back. We kept it in this little goldfish bowl—a few pebbles on the bottom, turtle food, and this little tiny turtle. Its whole existence was there, and I felt sorry for the poor thing. I felt confined by its confinement and finally talked my son into giving the turtle its freedom. He agreed, and we waited until spring, when the earth had warmed up and the streams were flowing. We took the turtle to the stream behind the house and made a big ceremony of tossing it into the stream and setting it free. The most remarkable thing happened with this docile creature that had always looked as if it were half dead. It rarely moved in the bowl; every once in a while its head would come out of the shell, but mostly it was hidden. The minute it hit the water, though, it swam like a fish. It went right to a rock and turned to face the oncoming stream. With its neck stuck out, it started this waving pattern, jutting out from either side of the rock, back and forth. What it was doing I later found out was feeding itself. That motion is how turtles catch the insects and debris washed down by the stream. He had never been in a stream before, but the moment the water touched his body, those forces triggered some kind of primordial truth of "turtle nature," which he manifested. He didn't know he was manifesting it, but what he was doing manifested the existence of an endless ancestry of turtles, and an endless future of turtles, somehow in his genes, in his being.

That's the way it is with ceaseless practice. It is raising the Bodhi mind, the realization of oneself, the actualization of one's self, and nirvana. "There is not the slightest gap: practice, enlightenment, nirvana. Ceaseless practice continually revolves." The word *ceaseless* is also translated as "continuous." When we think of something as being "continuous," we generally think of it as a kind of circle. But to really understand how this works, think of a spiral. Think of raising the Bodhi mind, practice, enlightenment, and nirvana as the circle almost closing itself. It is an upward spiral; so again, there is the raising of the Bodhi mind, again practice, again enlightenment, again nirvana, again and again. The spiral continues upward, downward, sideways; it is a spiral that moves through time and space.

"Ceaseless practice continually revolves. Therefore, it does not depend on individual powerful acts nor on the spirit of others. It is undefiled, ceaseless practice. The virtue of ceaseless practice maintains self and others. Essentially, our ceaseless practice fills heaven and earth, and influences everything with its virtue. Although we may be unaware of it, it still occurs."

"It does not depend on individual powerful acts, nor on the spirit of others." That is, only a Buddha can realize Buddha, only a Buddha can transmit to a Buddha. Only a bird can fly. Only a turtle knows how to do what a turtle does. Do you see? The virtue of our life is the possibility of realizing ourselves. The virtue of our life is that whether it

"OUR
CEASELESS
PRACTICE
FILLS
HEAVEN AND
EARTH."

is realized or not, the freedom that is the life of a Buddha is inherent. No "powerful act" needs to be done in order to have the Buddha nature. No "powerful act" needs to be performed in order to live the life of a Buddha, to eat the Buddha's food, wear the Buddha's clothes, sleep in the Buddha's bed. We do it all the time. "Although we may be unaware of it, it still occurs," *because* "ceaseless practice cannot be described as being hidden or revealed."

"Ceaseless practice is not in the places where the worldly seek, yet all must return to it. Through the ceaseless practice of Buddhas of the past, present, and future, all of the Buddhas of the past, present, and future emerge." When you manifest ceaseless practice, you manifest the life of all Buddhas past, present, and future. "The virtue of ceaseless practice is never hidden; therefore the mind is aroused and practice begins." It can't be hidden because it is vast and boundless; there is no place to hide it.

"Its virtue, however, is not immediately revealed and thus it cannot be seen, cannot be heard or comprehended." Why can't it be seen, heard, or comprehended? Because it is vast and boundless. In order to see it, hear it, or comprehend it, you have to move away from it. As long as there is ceaseless practice, there is only ceaseless practice. Ceaseless practice always exists this very moment. "Although it is not revealed, do not study it as something hidden." If you do, what you'll find yourself doing is searching for it. Although you are a Buddha and may not realize it, do not practice as if it were something hidden, because then you go looking for something outside yourself. That was the mistake that Joshu made when he asked Nansen, "What is the Way?" Nansen said, "Ordinary mind is the Way." Joshu said, "Shall I direct myself toward it or not?" Immediately, he was putting himself outside of it. To him, "ordinary mind" was something other than what he was. Nansen then told him, "If you direct yourself toward it, you move away from it." The same thing applies to

NO "POWER-
FUL ACT"
NEEDS TO BE
PERFORMED
TO LIVE THE
LIFE OF A
BUDDHA.
WE DO IT
ALL THE
TIME.

ceaseless practice. If you practice as if it is something hidden, you move farther and farther away from it.

"Since ceaseless practice cannot be described as hidden or revealed, manifested or submerged, we should not be concerned with knowing the cause of ceaseless practice. Indeed, such knowledge is nothing special. Causation, or cause and effect, is ceaseless practice. Ceaseless practice is not causation. We must study this in detail. Ceaseless practice which manifests ceaseless practice is nothing other than the ceaseless practice of the present." Cause and effect are one. The logic underlying the principle of "nonobstruction of phenomenon against phenomenon" in Hua Yen philosophy speaks to this point, as does the "mutual identity and mutual penetration of phenomena" as it was presented in that system of thought. You can see that mutual identity means the nondifferentiated state in which antitheses—such as one and many, absolute and relative, being and nonbeing, life and death, enlightenment and delusion—all coexist in oneness and interfusion. "Mutual penetration" refers to the simultaneous origination of all things and events interpenetrating one another in their myriad realms and dimensions.

> Since practice and the Way are neither large nor small, neither self nor other, neither existing previously nor just arising now, they therefore exist "thus." They are completely interpenetrated. As a result, their origination is simultaneous—they therefore exist "thus." Cause and effect is ceaseless practice; however, ceaseless practice is not cause and effect. The ceaseless practice which manifests ceaseless practice is none other than the ceaseless practice of this very moment. The single moment has no substance; it becomes interchangeable with great eons. Ten thousand kalpas *is* this very moment; this very moment is the ten thousand *kalpas*. Because the kalpas have no substance, they also embrace the single moment. Since both the single moment and the great kalpas

"WE SHOULD NOT BE CONCERNED WITH KNOWING THE CAUSE OF CEASELESS PRACTICE."

have no substance, all the marks of the long and the short merge into a great harmony. Hence, all the universes that are far away or nearby, all the Buddhas and sentient beings, and all the things and events in the past, present, and future come into view simultaneously. Since time is inseparable from events, if one moment becomes nonobstructive, all the dharmas will automatically be harmoniously merged. This is why all things and events in the past, present, and future vividly appear within one moment in time. When we penetrate a single dharma, we understand all dharmas. Unless we understand all dharmas thoroughly, we cannot apprehend a single dharma. When one understands the meaning of thoroughness and thereby penetrates thoroughly, one discerns all dharmas as well as a single dharma. For this reason, when one studies a single object, one learns the whole universe without fail.

This is Dogen expressing, "He who knows the single object comprehends the entire universe." The understanding of cause and effect always has to do with this very moment. Cause and effect are arranged, not in linear order, in terms of before and after, but as absolute events or moments discrete from each other, each abiding in its own dharma position. Cause is not before and effect is not after. "Cause is perfect and effect is perfect. Cause is nondual; dharma is nondual; effect is nondual. The effect is occasioned by cause. They are not before or after, because before and after are nondual in the Way." This is what Dogen calls "wondrous cause and effect."

Causation is ceaseless practice; ceaseless practice is not causation. We must study this in detail. Ceaseless practice which manifests ceaseless practice is nothing other than the ceaseless practice of the present. Cause and effect are one. What is that one? Ceaseless practice is neither past, present, nor future. Then what is it? Dogen says:

CEASELESS PRACTICE IS NEITHER PAST, PRESENT, NOR FUTURE.

> The ceaseless practice of the present is not the ceaseless practice of the original self. Nor does it come and

go, exit and enter. "In the present" does not mean existing prior to ceaseless practice. It refers to the time ceaseless practice emerges. That is why the ceaseless practice of one day, one moment, is the seed of all the Buddhas. Through ceaseless practice, all Buddhas are manifest and their ceaseless practice occurs. No ceaseless practice emerges when we despise the Buddhas, do not respect them, detest ceaseless practice, do not identify life and death with the Buddha, and do not study and practice. The present world of blooming flowers and falling leaves is the actualization of ceaseless practice. Polishing and then smashing a mirror is not different from ceaseless practice. Therefore, anyone who tries to escape from practice because of a malicious heart cannot do so; even that action is within ceaseless practice. Every moment we practice one dharma, we complete one dharma.

TO LIVE
OUR LIFE IS
TO PRAC-
TICE CEASE-
LESSLY
THE TEN
THOUSAND
THINGS.

There is no way to separate ourselves from the ten thousand things. The ten thousand things are our life itself. To live our life is to practice ceaselessly the ten thousand things, whether we realize it or not. When we realize it, we make ourselves free. When we don't realize it, although we are free, we bind ourselves. We put ourselves inside the cage and we lock the door. Then, rattling the bars, we cry out to be set free. All along, freedom is in our own hands, and all along the locks are on the inside of the cage, so no one else can let us out. Only we can do it. Someone else can tell you that you have the key, and you can "believe" that you have the way out, but until you actually unlock the door that is practice, there's no getting out of the cage. It can even be said that the cage doesn't exist; you just think it is there, and as a result it works like an invisible wall. I had a dog once that was not allowed in the dining room or living room of the house. The dog was very bright and very well trained. There were no gates; he was just told "No!" every time he went into the living room. When he was still a puppy he knew that there were two rooms that he wasn't allowed to go into. He really liked to fetch, and one time a visiting friend threw the ball right into the living room. The dog ran after it at full speed but slid to a full stop at the entrance as if he'd smashed up against a wall. There was an invisible wall there—invisible to everyone but the dog. He couldn't go another step farther but waited there at the threshold, whining and barking, his tail wagging, wanting to go get the ball but unable to because he was conditioned. That is the way the cage of the self is for all of us. Until we realize that we placed it there, we can't remove it and make ourselves free. It doesn't matter how much talking I do, how much the Buddhadharma and the sutras say and reveal, how much you believe. Believing doesn't cut it; understanding it doesn't cut it. It's only when you make it your own that you manifest the freedom of a Buddha.

"Hence from the ceaseless practice of all Buddhas and ancestors, our own ceaseless practice emerges, and we can attain the Great Way. From our own ceaseless practice, the ceaseless practice of all Buddhas emerges and all Buddhas attain the way." Isn't that interesting? Our action occurs because of the action of all previous Buddhas, and our action, simultaneously, creates the action of all previous Buddhas. Buddhas of the past, because of our action, can practice the Way. Buddhas of the future can, too. Because of our action, "it" moves through time to the past and to the future. Not only are we the effect of the Buddhas' and ancestors' enlightenment and practice, we are also the cause. Cause and effect are one.

CAUSE AND EFFECT ARE ONE.

"From our own ceaseless practice there is endless virtue. Accordingly, all the Buddhas and ancestors endlessly live as Buddha, transcend Buddha, have the mind of Buddha, and become Buddha." *Buddha* means "enlightened one" or "realized one." You should know that from the turtle's own ceaseless practice there is endless virtue. Accordingly, all turtles endlessly live as turtles, transcend turtles, have the mind of turtles, and become turtles. It is hard to say

57

that the turtle locked in the little bowl was really a turtle. He didn't do all the things that turtles do. He had never tasted the mountain stream, the coolness of the water. The bird in the cage had never felt the wind on its wings. It is hard to say that it was really a bird. So it is with sentient beings. We look like Buddha, act like Buddha, manifest the life of Buddha in our moment-to-moment existence, yet we haven't realized Buddha, and as such, we are not free. We are limited by circumstances, by cause and effect.

> Vast and boundless, nothing is hidden
> In clear water, all the way to the bottom
> The fish swims like a fish.
> Vast, limitless sky, transparent throughout
> The bird flies like a bird
> Extremely subtle and profound—
> How can I explain?

NO MATTER HOW FAR THAT BIRD FLIES, IT NEVER REACHES THE LIMITS OF ITS FLYING.

It is because it is vast and boundless with nothing hidden that the bird can fly like a bird and the fish can swim like a fish. There is no boundary. No matter how far that fish swims, it never reaches the limits of its medium. No matter how far that bird flies, it never reaches the limits of its flying. It is the same with all beings. No creature, vast or small, ever falls short of its own completeness, ever fails to cover the ground upon which it stands. But how can this be explained?

> The tiny snowflakes
> They fall no place but here—
> Is this the passing of fall,
> Or the appearance of winter?
> . . . Tiny snowflakes
> They fall no place but here.
> Do you understand?

PART TWO
Solitary Peak

7

MOUNTAINS AND RIVERS

TODAY I would like to read a passage from *The Moun-tains and Rivers Sutra* of the great Soto master Dogen Zenji:

> The Master Ta-yang, addressing the assembly, said, "The blue mountains are constantly walking; the stone woman gives birth to a child in the night." The mountains lack nothing, hence they are constantly at rest and constantly walking. We must devote our-selves to a detailed study of this virtue of walking. The walking of the mountains is like that of people; do not doubt that mountains walk simply because they may not appear to walk like humans. These words of the Patriarch Ta-yang point out the funda-mental meaning of walking, and we should thorough-ly investigate his teaching on "constant walking." Because the blue mountains are walking, they are constant. Their walk is swifter than the wind; yet those in the mountains do not sense this, do not know it. To be "in the mountains" is a flower opening in the world. Those without eyes to see the mountains do not sense, do not know, do not see, do not hear this truth. [They] who doubt that mountains walk do not yet understand [their] own walking. It is that [they do] not yet understand, have not yet made clear, [their] walking. He who would understand his own walking must also understand the walking of the blue mountains. The blue mountains are neither sentient

nor insentient; the self is neither sentient nor insentient. Therefore, we can have no doubts about these blue mountains walking.

On Easter Sunday we did a memorial service for Monsignor Scully, the builder of our monastery. In our tradition it is customary to write a memorial poem for this service, addressed to the person who has died. The poem this time was:

> Mountain of heavenly light is constantly walking.
> A stone woman gives birth to a son in the night.
> When mountain flowers open here,
> The Nazarene rises and enters the market.
> How can we express our gratitude?

WHEN WE HEAR THIS KIND OF THING, IT SHAKES THE MIND.

Mountains walking, stone women giving birth, the Nazarene arising, sentient/insentient, inside/outside—when we hear this kind of thing, it shakes the mind. As we try to grasp it with our logical sequential way of dealing with reality, it doesn't compute; it creates a kind of short-circuit. We try to get around it by thinking, "Mountains walking . . . that must be some kind of poetic expression, some kind of romanticism." Dogen, however, was not being romantic or poetic—he was describing reality. He was coming from the point of view of what is real. It depends on how you see, as he said. *Because the blue mountains are walking, they are constant. Their walk is swifter than the wind, yet those in the mountains do not sense this, do not know it. To be "in the mountains" is a flower opening within the world. Those outside the mountains do not sense this, do not know it. Those without eyes to see the mountains do not sense, do not know, do not see, do not hear this truth.*

Some years ago after the completion of the book *The Way of Everyday Life* (on Dogen Zenji's *Genjokoan*), for which Maezumi Roshi did commentaries and I did photographs, we talked about working on *The Mountains and Rivers Sutra* next. I began studying the sutra and working with him on it, and then I started photographing it. When

I climbed a mountain with all my photographic equipment and looked around, I began to realize that nothing I photographed would look like "mountain." You have to be off the mountain to photograph it; when you are "in the mountain," there is no mountain.

It is the same with everything we experience. When you are the anger, the fear, or whatever the barrier is, it disappears. When you are the barrier, there is no barrier. It is only when we separate ourselves from it that it appears. When we base our life on the illusion of separation, all the complications appear and we look outside ourselves for the cause of our unhappiness. Your job is rotten. Your luck is terrible. Your boss made you angry. But your boss did not make you angry; only you can make you angry. When you begin to realize that there is no outside or inside, that what you do and what happens to you are the same thing, then the way you solve that problem is very different. How can you separate yourself? You are it. You are the cause and you are the effect; you create it and you can put it to rest. To understand this talk of mountains and rivers we need to understand "no separation." When you experience the fact that what you do and what happens to you are the same thing, you return to reality.

The blue mountains are neither sentient nor insentient; the self is neither sentient nor insentient. Dogen presents an unusual view of nature. In one of his discourses on dharma, he speaks of insentient beings in an extraordinary way:

> The way insentient beings expound dharma should not be understood to be necessarily like the way sentient beings expound dharma. The voices of sentient beings should follow the principle of their discourse on dharma. Even so, it is contrary to the Buddha Way to usurp the voices of the living and conjecture about those of the nonliving in terms of them—even though people's judgment now tries to recognize grasses and trees and the like, and liken them to nonliving things, they too cannot be measured by the ordinary mind.

63

Insentient beings are often conceived of as comprising the physical universe—what we call "nature," and think of as really dead, nonliving. People unwittingly or romantically anthropomorphize nature, but think that nature is insentient. To put it another way, we draw a boundary between sentient and insentient, perceiving and judging each in a particular way. Dogen rejects such a conception of nature. From the standpoint of the Way, insentient beings do elucidate dharma—not in human language, but in their own expressions—hence they are alive in their own way. What Dogen is saying is that insentient beings are sentient, sentient beings insentient—no separation. When we perceive reality in terms of the separation that begins with the boundary between self and other, we extend this perception to everything else—good and bad, up and down, heaven and earth, heads and tails, black and white. Yet every one of these dualities is two parts of the same reality—not two separate things. How can you have the idea of "good" without the idea of "bad"? How can we talk about "up" unless there is a "down"? They are mutually arising, co-dependent. Heads and tails are two parts of the same reality—you cannot have one without the other. That is a very different way of looking at the world—and of looking at yourself and others. If you are seeing from the point of view of that co-dependence, of the absolute, seeing yourself and others as two parts of the same reality, then "the blue mountains walking" and "the stone woman giving birth in the night" do not sound so strange.

Master Su T'ung-p'o, who was a poet, listened to the discourse on insentient beings and sentient beings but could never quite understand the full significance of it. One night he was suddenly awakened by the sounds of the mountain streams flowing in the silence of the night. This was the moment of his enlightenment. He composed the following poem:

> Sounds of the brooks are nothing but a great tongue;
> The forms of mountains are none other than

INSENTIENT
BEINGS DO
ELUCIDATE
DHARMA.

Buddha's body of Purity;
Eighty-four thousand gathas [verses] since last night.
How shall I explain them tomorrow!

The night when this poet was enlightened by the sounds of the mountain streams, they struck him as if raging waves were soaring in the sky. Thus the sound of the streams awakening Su T'ung-p'o is the working of the brook sounds, their discourse flowing into the poet's ears. Dogen says: "I suspect that the talk on the sermon of insentient beings is still reverberating, may be secretly intermingling with the nightly sounds of the streams. Can anyone say that this is a pint of water, or an ocean to which all rivers enter? Ultimately speaking, is it the poet that is enlightened? He who has a discerning eye should apprehend the great tongue and the body of purity. Was it the sound of the river that enlightened the poet, or did the poet enlighten the sound?"

When there is no separation, how can you speak from one point of view or the other? What the poet realized was no separation. So who was enlightened—he or the sound of the streams? Who is it that walks—you or the mountain? What is "mountain walking"? What is "the stone woman giving birth in the night"? The flower opens on this mountain; the Nazarene rises and enters the market. The flower opening that Dogen refers to and that I refer to in the poem is the flower that Shakyamuni held up before an assembly of a thousand of his followers. That was his whole sermon, the holding up of a flower. Only Mahakashyapa, who was in the audience, smiled. In that moment Shakyamuni transmitted the marvelous mind of nirvana. That same mind-to-mind transmission has continued for 2,500 years. It continues today.

WHAT IS "MOUNTAIN WALKING"? WHAT IS "THE STONE WOMAN GIVING BIRTH IN THE NIGHT"?

The flower opening is realization. At that same moment of realization the carpenter arises from the dead and enters the marketplace, just as the blue mountains walk and the stone woman gives birth to a child in the middle of the

You can-
not under-
stand it
with your
head.

night. Do you understand? You can not understand in your head, with your intellect. The only way to penetrate this is to be it. The only way to penetrate a barrier, a wall that obstructs you, or your koan is to *be* it! When you become it, the ten thousand things return to the self, where they have always been.

I would like to end this chapter with a poem of Han Shan, the hermit monk who lived on Ko Mountain in China at the end of the eighth century:

A thing to be valued—this famed mountain;
How can the Seven treasures compare?
Pines and moonlight, breezy and cool;
Clouds and mist, ragged wisps rising,
Clustering around it, how many folds of hills?
Twisting back and forth, how many miles of trails?
Valley streams quiet, limpid and clear
Joys and delights that never end!

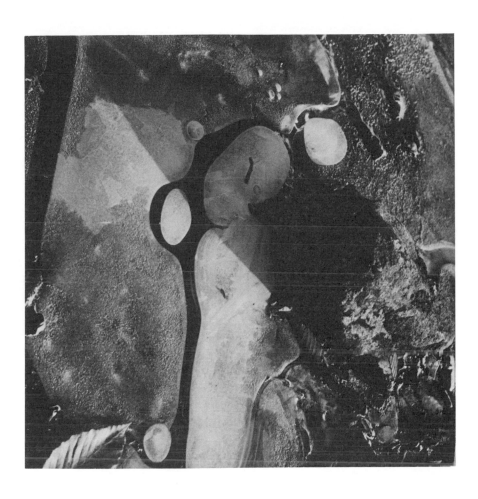

8

"The Sound of Rain"

Blue Cliff Record: Case 46

WITH A SINGLE STROKE he completes it and passes beyond ordinary and holy. His slightest word can break things up, untying what is bound and releasing what is stuck. As if walking on thin ice or running over sword blades, he sits within the heaps of sound and form. He walks on top of sound and form. For the moment, I leave aside wondrous functioning in all directions. How is it when he leaves that very instant? To test, I cite this old case. Listen!

MAIN CASE

Kyosei asked a monk, "What is that sound outside the gate?" The monk said, "The sound of raindrops." Kyosei said, "Sentient beings are inverted, they lose themselves and follow after things." The monk said, "What about you, Teacher?" Kyosei said, "I almost don't lose myself." The monk said, "What is the meaning of 'I almost don't lose myself'?" Kyosei said, "Though it still should be easy to express oneself, to say the whole thing has to be difficult."

SOLITARY PEAK

VERSE

An empty hall, the sound of raindrops
Hard to respond, even for an adept.
If you say he has ever let the streams enter,
As before you still don't understand.
Understanding or not understanding
On the south mountain,
On the north mountain
More and more downpour.

Kyosei, one of the leading teachers of ancient Chinese Zen, was a successor to Master Seppo, who succeeded Master Tokusan. In another famous koan, "Kyosei's Pecking and Tapping," he uses the image of the pecking and tapping between the mother hen and her chick inside the egg. When the chick is ready to come forth, it begins tapping on the inside of the shell, and the hen, hearing this, responds: *peck, peck, peck.* Sometimes the hen starts, *peck, peck, peck.* And the chick responds, *tap, tap, tap.* It's *peck, tap, peck, tap*—the two of them working together bring the chick out of the shell into the world. Kyosei often utilized this image to elucidate his particular style of teaching and to point out that the relationship between hen and chick, teacher and student, is critically timed. If the pecking starts too soon, instead of a chick, what "hatches" is an undeveloped embryo. If it starts too late, the chick can smother inside the egg. Hence, it is vitally important that what happens is a well-coordinated effort between teacher and student, hen and chick. In this case the teacher leads, the hen taps. *What is that sound outside the gate?* Kyosei says, stirring it up. In his pointer, Engo is referring to Kyosei in saying: *With a single stroke he completes it and passes beyond ordinary and holy.* We should look closely at what is meant by this phrase "ordinary and holy." Chanting the sutras, chopping wood—how do you do it, how do you use your mind? Dogen said, "Those who regard the mundane as a hindrance to practice only understand that in the mundane there is nothing

CHANTING THE SUTRAS, CHOPPING WOOD—HOW DO YOU DO IT?

70

sacred. They do not yet understand that in sacredness, nothing is mundane." *His slightest word can break things up, untying what is bound and releasing what is stuck.* That's what is going on with the monk in this koan—he is "stuck." *As if walking on thin ice, or running over sword blades, he sits within heaps of sound and form. He walks on top of sound and form.* Kyosei, however, is not led around by it; he has completely mastered it.

Kyosei asks the monk, "What is that sound outside the gate?" Engo's footnote says, *He casually lets down a hook.* Obviously, Kyosei doesn't suffer from deafness; what is he asking? "What is that sound outside?" The monk says, "It's the sound of raindrops." Why did Kyosei ask that question? Nothing is extra in a koan; every line is teaching. It is trimmed down to the very heart of the matter. That's why Engo points out what is going on in his footnote, *He casually lets down a hook.* He is out to catch a fish, and the fish is the monk.

NOTHING IS EXTRA IN A KOAN; EVERY LINE IS TEACHING.

The monk said, "The sound of raindrops." Engo's footnote says, *He's undeniably truthful; it's good news, too.* Kyosei says, "Sentient beings are inverted. They are upside down. They lose themselves and follow after things." The footnote: *A concern is born. Kyosei is used to getting his way. He rakes the monk in. He depends on his own abilities.* To be "inverted, upside down," to "lose oneself" and "follow after things" is being controlled by circumstances, not taking responsibility. You can hear it in statements such as, "It's his fault," "She made me angry," "I didn't do it; he did it."

The monk said, "What about you, Teacher?" Engo's footnote reads: *As it turns out, the monk suffers a defeat. He's turned the spear around. Inevitably, it will be hard for Kyosei to stand up to it.* What he has done is kind of tricky. He has taken the question and turned it back on the teacher. The monk "grabs the spear" and stabs at Kyosei. Kyosei says, "I almost don't lose myself." He doesn't say, "I don't lose myself." Or, "I never lose myself." He says, "I *almost* don't lose myself." The footnote says, *Bah! He just can't explain.*

71

The monk says, "What is the meaning of 'I almost don't lose myself'?" This monk keeps pressing. The footnote says, *He presses this old fellow and crushes the man, his first arrow was still light. The second arrow was deep.* Kyosei said, "Though it still should be easy to express oneself, to say the whole thing has to be difficult." Engo's footnote says, *Provisions to nourish a son. Although it is like this, where have Tokusan and Rinzai gone? If he doesn't call it the sound of raindrops, what sound shall he call it? It simply can't be explained.*

That answer, of course, would not be acceptable in the interview room. "What is that sound outside?" "I can't explain it." Then don't explain—show it! Reveal it! Engo asks, "Where have Tokusan and Rinzai gone?" because were either of these two masters questioned in this way, immediately the stick would have come down across the monk's back or a great *"Hough!"* would have been shouted out. But Kyosei was a compassionate, grandmotherly sort of teacher who hand-fed the monk; he would have chewed it up and swallowed it for him if he could. Somehow, the monk still didn't get it. Engo says in his commentary, "You should understand right here that when the ancient adepts imparted their teaching with one device, one object, they wanted to guide people."

One day Kyosei asked a monk, "What is the sound outside the gate?" The monk said, "The sound of a quail." Kyosei said, "If you wish to avoid uninterrupted hell, don't slander the wheel of the true dharma of the Tathagatha." How did the monk "slander the dharma of the Tathagatha" by saying it was the sound of a quail? Kyosei asked another monk, "What is that sound outside the gate?" The monk said, "The sound of a snake eating a frog." Kyosei said, "I knew that sentient beings suffer; here is another suffering sentient being." This is the same thing that is going on in this case. Why does he say that "I knew that sentient beings suffer; here is another suffering sentient being"? It is a beautiful way to respond to that monk's problem.

DON'T
EXPLAIN—
SHOW IT!

The monk was separating himself. His head was filled with ideas about things. All three of the monks in these examples had the same problem. When you separate yourself, you suffer. The cause of suffering is the delusion that there exists a separate self to begin with. Those are the first teachings of the Buddha: life is suffering; the cause of suffering is thirst or desire. Desire is born of the illusion of separation, because when you separate yourself, when you put yourself inside that bag of skin, everything else in the universe is left out. What you've got is a bag of bones, meat, blood, and organs—is that who you are? If it is, then everything you need is to be found somewhere outside the skin bag. And that, in itself, is the cause of suffering. It gives rise to all the dualities, such as gain and loss, love and hate, good and bad, up and down. Greed, anger, ignorance—what Buddhism calls the three poisons—are based on the illusion of separation. When the self is forgotten, greed, anger, and ignorance are transformed into compassion, wisdom, and realization.

THE CAUSE OF SUFFERING IS THE DELUSION THAT THERE EXISTS A SEPARATE SELF.

Engo said, "If students of Zen can penetrate here, nothing can block their independence within heaps of sound and form. If you can't penetrate here, then you are constrained by sound and form." Kyosei's words in this case are also called "penetrating sound and form" or "explaining the eye of the path," or "explaining sound and form," or "explaining the mind source," or "explaining forgetting feelings, forgetting preaching." These are nice interpretations, but they are all clichés. They don't really reach it. The idea is wonderful, but it is not the thing. The explanation is marvelous, but it is not the thing. The thing itself, not the ideas and words that describe it, is what is necessary.

A number of years ago we had a student here who was quite a famous musician who traveled all over the world giving concerts, and was very well regarded by his peers and by the critics. He was very interested in this koan, "The Sound of Rain," and kept wanting to work on it. One day during Dharma Combat he came forward and said that hpe wanted to work on it, so I asked him, "What is the sound of rain?" He said, "I can't hear, I can't hear anything." I said, "Come a little closer." He came forward, and I said, "You can hear." You see, "I can't hear anything" is an idea. Not hearing is not an idea. Being one with the thing itself is transcending hearing and seeing. Being the thing itself is "No eye, ear, nose, tongue, body, mind / No color sound, smell, taste, touch, phenomena / No world of sight / No world of consciousness." That's what it means when Dogen Zenji says, "Hearing sounds with the whole body and mind / Seeing forms with the whole body and mind / One understands them intimately." No separation—no self, no other.

"No eye, ear, nose, tongue, body, mind."

When Kyosei asked, "What is that sound outside the gate?" and the monk said, "The sound of raindrops," immediately Kyosei said, "Sentient beings are upside down, they're inverted. They lose themselves and follow after things." He was pointing to that separation. A lot of people misinterpret Kyosei's response as intentionally upsetting the man, "trying to pull the rug out." That has nothing to do with it. The rug was already out the minute he opened his mouth. Old Kyosei was just an innocent old grandmother watching the whole thing come down and desperately trying to help him. He's a very courageous old grandmother, too. He isn't bound by a single device or object. Engo says of him, "Above all, he doesn't spare his eyebrows." That refers to an image in one of the sutras, and a case in *The Blue Cliff Record* called "Zuigan's Eyebrows." It is said that if you put out bad dharma, you lose your eyebrows. Also, if you "expound it completely," you lose your eyebrows. That is why Zuigan, after an *ango* (three-month Zen training intensive) at his monastery, asked, "I've been speaking to you during this whole *ango*, giving dharma talks every week. Do I have my eyebrows or not?" One of the monks yelled, "A robber is in a funk!" Another monk said, "They've grown." Unmon, who was one of the monks at that time, said, "Barrier!" So old Kyosei

74

doesn't mind losing his eyebrows, doesn't mind "slopping around in the mud." Bad dharma is sometimes put out just for the sake of all sentient beings, because the moment a teacher opens his mouth, the moment he points, he is "fouling the nest"—and he knows it. But out of great compassion, Kyosei chases after this monk, trying to feed him.

How could Kyosei not have known that it was the sound of raindrops? Why was it still worth asking? He was using his probing pole to check the depths, to examine the monk. That constant testing is very important. Students sometimes come to an interview and say, "If I don't have any questions, should I still come?" Of course. The interview is the place where we test each other. I want to know how your sitting is, what your realization is, what you've seen. And to keep you on the track—it's very easy to go astray, to get caught up in your own *makyo,* your own hallucinations or illusions, and run around calling them "it." "This is it, I've got it!" The minute you say, "I've got it," you miss it. It is not an idea, not a concept. The minute you've "got it," you've separated yourself. In order to get it, you need the getter and the thing that the getter is getting. Two. The dharma is not two. But the monk pressed right back, saying, "What about you, Teacher?" What happened then is that this sweet, compassionate old teacher went into the mud and said to him, "I almost don't lose myself." The reason for his saying this is that the monk was losing himself; he was actively engaged in pursuing things. Why did Kyosei lose himself, too? You can't talk back and forth, you can't communicate, unless you're communicating in the same language. In order to teach devils, you need to manifest as a devil. In order to teach gods, you need to manifest as a god. Devils can't teach gods, and gods can't teach devils. No separation. That is the great, compassionate heart of Avalokiteshvara Bodhisattva.

The monk was dull. He wanted to beat the statement to the ground. Already it was exhausted, the stink of Zen was emanating everywhere, but the monk wouldn't let go. "What is the meaning of 'I almost don't lose myself'?" Can

THE MINUTE YOU SAY, "I'VE GOT IT," YOU MISS IT.

DEVILS CAN'T TEACH GODS, AND GODS CAN'T TEACH DEVILS.

75

you imagine what would have happened if Tokusan had been asked a question like that? He used to beat the monks who came to him. If they were right, he would hit them; if they were wrong, he would hit them. If they were neither right nor wrong, he would hit them. Thirty blows. They used to be terrified; they wouldn't come through the door to his room. He would be sitting in there with a stick, waiting for them. Can you imagine what old Tokusan would have done with this monk intent on running things to the ground! The blows and the shouts would have been falling all over the place before his mouth even opened.

But not Kyosei. He put out a beautiful path for him, followed him like an old grandmother, and created complications along the way. "Though it still should be easy to express oneself, to say the whole thing has to be difficult." Kyosei was trying to show this monk the great affair right under his feet. It is above our heads, under our feet. If you call it the sound of rain, you're blind. If you don't call it the sound of rain, what will you call it? Your feet need to be on the ground of reality, the ground of being, before you can get in here. What was the meaning of "I almost don't lose myself"? Why didn't he say, "I never lose myself" or "I don't lose myself"? Why "I *almost* don't lose myself"?

DOES THE SOUND COME TO THE EAR, OR DOES THE EAR GO TO THE SOUND? The sound of rain—does the sound come to the ear, or does the ear go to the sound? This is the same as the question of life and death. The same as absolute and relative. Being "upside down" means being deluded by the self, following after things. Where are the things to pursue? What are the things? They only exist outside ourselves when we place them there by the way we use our mind.

> An empty hall, the sound of raindrops.
> Hard to respond, even for an adept.
> If you say he has ever let the streams enter
> As before, you still don't understand.

If you call it the sound of rain, then this is losing yourself and following after things. If you don't call it the sound of rain, then how do you turn it around? At this point, even if you are an adept, it is hard to respond. Engo says, "Therefore, an ancient master said that if your view equals your teacher's, you have less than half your teacher's merit. Only if your view goes beyond your teacher's are you fit to receive and carry on the transmission."

> Understanding or not understanding
> On the south mountain,
> On the north mountain
> More and more downpour.

It isn't easy, and yet it is so simple: just take responsibility, just don't separate yourself from the ten thousand things. Once that step happens, the ten thousand things return to the self—where they have always been, and where they are right now, regardless of whether we realize it or not. Because of our conditioning, we separate ourselves, we lock ourselves in this bag of skin and call it a self, and place everything else outside it and call it "other." Self and other are not two.

We are the lucky ones: we have a process, a way, a direction, a path, for turning that "upside-downness" right side up. We have a way to illuminate that darkness. Ignorance, or delusion, means darkness, having no light, not knowing what is real. The illusion of the self as a separate entity is what is not real. When that basic premise is where you start from, then everything else that follows is equally not real. When the first thought springs from enlightenment, from the realization that the self is empty, then all subsequent thoughts are enlightened.

WE LOCK OURSELVES IN THIS BAG OF SKIN.

We are free, every one of us. We are born free, and the bondage, restrictions, and limits that we find in our life are self-created. The edges we perceive have been placed there by the way we use our minds. There are fundamentally no edges, no boundaries. But this practice has nothing to do with believing. We don't have Zen believers. It also has nothing to do with understanding. Understanding implies a separation between the knower and the thing that the knower knows. It has to do with the direct and intimate experience itself. Your experience. Not Shakyamuni Buddha's, not mine—yours. Only you can make yourself free. No one can do it for you. The only one with the power to do it is you yourself. "Only a Buddha can realize Buddha"—and it is nowhere to be found other than on top of the seat that you're sitting on.

> If you can hear with your eye
> And see with your ear,
> Then you will not doubt
> The raindrops dripping from the eaves.

9

The Goddess's "Neither Male Nor Female"

OF SHARIPUTRA it can be said that if you call him a man, you are caught up in the words and ideas that describe reality and you will miss the truth. If you call him a woman, you negate the fact—that, too, misses the truth. Without resorting to speech or silence, what do you call it? As for the Goddess, she doesn't know either. If you examine this carefully, you will see she is just a puppet on a string. Listen to the following.

Main Case

Shariputra asked the Goddess of the House of Vimalakirti, "What prevents you from transforming yourself out of your female state?" The Goddess said, "Although I have sought my female state for these twelve years, I have not yet found it. If a magician were to incarnate a woman by magic, would you ask her, 'What prevents you from transforming yourself out of your female state?'?" Shariputra said, "No, such a woman would not really exist, so what would there be to transform?" The Goddess said, "Just so, venerable Shariputra, all things do not really exist." The Goddess then exchanged form with Shariputra and asked, "Now, what prevents you from transforming out of your

"ALTHOUGH I HAVE SOUGHT MY FEMALE STATE FOR THESE TWELVE YEARS, I HAVE NOT FOUND IT."

81

female state?" Shariputra said, "I do not know what to transform." The Goddess said, "In all things there is neither male nor female, nor is there an end to male and female. Where do you find yourself?"

VERSE

Ever the same,
The moon among the clouds,
Different from each other,
The mountain and the valley.
Isn't it wonderful?
Isn't it miraculous?
Is this one, or is it two?

Vimalakirti was a famous lay practitioner who lived at the time of the Buddha, and his understanding was said to equal that of the Buddha. The *Vimalakirti Sutra* is a collection of his teachings, and one of the standard Mahayana sutras. Vimalakirti got very ill, and the Buddha asked his chief disciples to visit him. It seemed that Vimalakirti's sickness was "the sickness of all sentient beings." In his house—this was a kind of magical house—there were hundreds of thousands of bodhisattvas, disciples, and all sorts of deities who appeared and disappeared while they manifested the teachings. This particular chapter on the Goddess begins with Manjushri asking Vimalakirti, "How should a bodhisattva regard all living beings?" Vimalakirti replies, "A bodhisattva should regard all living beings as a wise person regards the reflection of the moon in the water or as magicians regard people created by magic. They should regard them as being like a face in the mirror, like the water of a mirage, like the sound of an echo, like a mass of clouds in the sky, like the previous moment of a ball of foam, like the appearance and disappearance of a bubble of water, like the core of the plantain tree, like a flash of lightning, like the fifth great element, like the seventh sense medium, like the appearance of matter in an

"REGARD ALL LIVING BEINGS AS A WISE PERSON REGARDS THE REFLECTION OF THE MOON IN THE WATER."

immaterial realm, like the sprout from a rotten seed, like a tortoise-hair coat, like fun and games of one who wishes to die, like the egoistic views of a stream winner, like the third rebirth of a once returner, like the descendant of a nonreturner, like the existence of desire, hatred, and folly in the saint, like the inhalation and exhalation of an ascetic absorbed in a meditation on cessation, like the tracks of a bird in the sky, like the erection of a eunuch, like the pregnancy of a barren woman, like dream-visions seen after waking, like the passions of one who is free of conceptualizations, like fire burning without fuel, like the reincarnation of one who has obtained ultimate liberation."

". . . LIKE THE TRACKS OF A BIRD IN THE SKY."

This same statement comes up later as the day progresses and the dialogue continues between Manjushri and Vimalakirti. Present at this gathering are all of the disciples of the Old School. The Old School is the Hinayana school, the original teaching. One of the things that Mahayana Buddhism has done is to shed a very different light on some of the Hinayana teachings. One such Hinayana teaching was, for example, that monks shouldn't wear any kind of adornment, such as flowers and the like. Another was that in order to become enlightened, a woman had to be reborn as a man. This is what comes up with the appearance of the Goddess.

Thereupon a certain Goddess who lived in that house, having heard this teaching of the dharma and being delighted, pleased, and overjoyed, manifested herself in the material body and showered the great spiritual heroes, the bodhisattvas, and the great disciples with heavenly flowers. When the flowers fell on the bodies of the bodhisattvas, they fell off onto the floor. But when they fell on the bodies of the great disciples, they stuck to them and did not fall. The great disciples shook the flowers and even tried to use their magical powers, but still the flowers would not shake off. Then the Goddess said, "Venerable Shariputra, why do you shake these flowers?" Shariputra replied, "Goddess, these flowers are not proper for our religious purpose, so we are trying to shake them off." The Goddess said, "Do not say that, venerable Shariputra. Why? These flowers are proper indeed. Why? Such flowers have neither constructual thought nor discrimination. But the elder Shariputra has both thought and discrimination. Venerable Shariputra, impropriety for one who has renounced the world for the discipline of the rightly taught dharma consists of constructual thought and discrimination, yet the elders are full of such thoughts. One who is without such thoughts is always proper. Venerable Shariputra, see how these flowers do not stick to the bodies of the bodhisattvas. This is because they have eliminated constructual thought and discrimination."

What is beginning to evolve in this koan is the difference between the emerging Mahayana teachings and those of the Hinayana school. The bodhisattva is a tradition in Mahayana Buddhism but not in Hinayana. In Hinayana the aim is total renunciation of the world; in Mahayana the dharma is manifested in the world. The venerable Shariputra said to the Goddess, "How long have you been in this house?" The Goddess replied, "I have been here as long as the elder has been in liberation." Shariputra said, "Then you have been in this house for quite some time." The Goddess said, "Has the elder been in liberation for quite some time?" At that the elder Shariputra fell silent. The Goddess continued, "Elder, you are foremost of the wise; why do you not speak? Now, when it is your turn, you do not answer the question." Shariputra was known as the foremost of all of the Buddha's disciples, the "wisest of the wise." He said, "Since liberation is inexpressible, Goddess, I do not know what to say."

Also in this sutra there is a point at which Vimalakirti falls silent that is regarded as an important teaching. Here, when Shariputra falls silent, the Goddess goes after him. "All of the syllables pronounced by the elder have the nature of liberation. Liberation is neither internal nor external, nor can it be apprehended apart from them. Like-

IN MAHAYANA BUDDHISM THE DHARMA IS MANIFESTED IN THE WORLD.

wise, symbols are neither internal nor external, nor can they be apprehended any place else. Therefore, Shariputra, do not point to liberation by abandoning speech." This dialogue continues on a little further until we get to the main case of the koan itself. "Goddess," Shariputra asks, "what prevents you from transforming yourself out of the female state?" He is specifically referring to the Hinayana teaching that enlightenment can be obtained only by men, that women must first reincarnate in the male form to reach the highest goal. Thus, Shariputra cannot understand why the Goddess would not use her extraordinary powers to become a man so that she could become enlightened.

This is an opportunity for the Goddess to teach. She says, "Although I have sought my female state for these twelve years, I have not yet found it. If a magician were to incarnate a woman by magic, would you ask her, 'What prevents you from transforming yourself out of your female state?'?" Shariputra says, "No, such a woman would not really exist, so what would there be to transform?" The Goddess replies, "Just so, venerable Shariputra, all things do not really exist." The Goddess then employs her magical powers to cause the elder Shariputra to appear in her form and to cause herself to appear in Shariputra's form. The Goddess transformed into Shariputra says to Shariputra transformed into the Goddess, "Venerable Shariputra, what prevents you from transforming out of your female state?" Shariputra, transformed into the Goddess, replies, "I no longer appear in the form of a male; my body has changed into the body of a woman. I do not know what to transform." The Goddess continues, "If the elder could change out of the female state, then all women could also change out of their female states. All women appear in the form of women in just the same way the elder appears in the form of a woman. While they are not women in reality, they appear in the form of women. With this in mind the Buddha said that in all things there is neither male nor female."

THIS IS AN OPPORTUNITY FOR THE GODDESS TO TEACH.

Then the Goddess releases her magical power and both return to their ordinary forms. She then says, "Venerable Shariputra, what have you done with your female form?" Shariputra says, "I neither made it nor did I change it." The Goddess says, "Just so, all things are neither made nor changed. That they are not made and not changed is the teaching of the Buddha." Shariputra says, "Where will you be born after you transmigrate after death?" The Goddess says, "I will be born where all magical incarnations of Tathagata are born." Shariputra says, "But the eminent incarnations of Tathagata do not transmigrate, nor are they born." The Goddess says, "All things and living beings are just the same; they do not transmigrate nor are they born."

This last exchange between Shariputra and the Goddess refers to the very last chapter of the *Diamond Sutra*. There is a beautiful little poem that sums up the teaching of the *Diamond Sutra*. In it the Buddha says, "Thus shall you regard all things—a flash of lightning in a summer sky, a bubble in a stream, a phantom and a dream." We need to look at what we mean when we say "reality." In Buddhist psychology there are eight levels of consciousness. The Buddhist way of understanding the totality of human experience is based on the fact that the organs of perception (eyes, ears, nose, tongue, body, and mind) and the objects of perception (form, sound, smell, taste, touch, and thought) give rise to visual, auditory, olfactory, gustatory, tactile, and mental consciousness and thus together create what we call "reality." When you sleep and dream you may go through all of the experiences of reality in that dream. You may dream that you are being chased by someone, and in the dream you break out into a sweat, you are out of breath, panting—suddenly the shock of the dream will bring you into wakefulness. Then you say, "Whew, that was only a dream; it was only my mind that was doing that." I tell you *this* is only a dream; *this* is only "your mind doing that." That is the teaching of the Buddha. What is real? What is reality? What is truth? Who are you?

I TELL YOU THIS IS ONLY A DREAM.

86

Each of the six levels of consciousness needs an object of perception. In the case of mind, the object of perception is thought. The thought may be a dream, an idea, an opinion, or something that has been "programmed" into you. When you combine that with consciousness, you have what we call reality. What you believe and what you think is who you are; it is what you manifest. That is why it is necessary to get underneath that program. You practice zazen to make yourself empty, to peel back the layers of conditioning of parents, teachers, and culture and to reach that ground of being. Underneath all of those layers is a person—that's what is to be realized. Once having realized it, we begin manifesting our life out of this realization, not out of the preconditioned ideas that have been fed to us. Every single one of us is conditioned from birth in one way or another, and that conditioning defines our life whether we like it or not. The conditioning is largely arbitrary, yet by the time we reach adulthood, we find ourselves functioning like robots. We don't know who we are, what our life is, or what its direction is. The liberation of the Buddha is to find that ground of being, to experience it intimately, and out of that experience to manifest one's life.

Of Shariputra it can be said that if you call him a man, you are caught up in the words and ideas that describe reality and you will miss the truth. If you call him a woman, you negate the fact. That, too, misses the truth. Without resorting to speech or silence, what do you call it? This is the standard difficulty we have in dealing with the dichotomies. Our minds are basically dualistic. It boggles the mind when we find statements like "Form is emptiness, emptiness is form; form is exactly emptiness, emptiness is exactly form." We cannot grasp it. The left hemisphere of the brain is linear and discursive and always creates separation. In actual fact, *it* is neither form nor emptiness. Then what is it? This is where the truth lies. Holding up a stick, the master says: It's neither a stick nor not a stick—what is it? There are hundreds of koans that deal with this point. How do you resolve it?

WHAT YOU BELIEVE AND WHAT YOU THINK IS WHO YOU ARE.

WHATEVER
THE KOAN
IS, WHATEV-
ER THE DIF-
FICULTY IS,
THERE IS
ONLY ONE
WAY
THROUGH
IT: BE IT.

Whatever the barrier is, whatever the koan is, whatever the difficulty is, there is only one way through it: *be* it. Whether we are talking about the koan Mu or the barrier of fear, the problem comes from separation. When we place the barrier or the difficulty outside of ourselves, we avoid taking responsibility, and when we don't take responsibility, there isn't anything we can really do about the problem. It is somebody else's fault and thus unsolvable. All we can do is whine about it or be frightened about it or run from it—from this illusion that we have created with our mind. That is why it is so vital to reach that ground of being, to realize personally that nothing is separate from ourselves. How do you do that? Be the barrier, be the fear, be Mu, be the koan, be the Goddess, be Shariputra.

How can you be the barrier? As long as you think that the bag of skin is who you are, you will never do it. When you realize that the bag of skin is the smallest part of who you are and what your life is, then there is nothing restricting you. There are no boundaries. Whether you realize it or not, there are no boundaries, but until you realize it you cannot manifest it. The limitations that each one of us has are defined by the ways we use our minds. Nothing changes in enlightenment—it is the same world before and after, the same you before and after. What changes is how you use your mind, how you perceive yourself, how you perceive the universe. That perception makes the difference between a life of pain, frustration, and ignorance and a life of peace and harmony with yourself and your environment, regardless of what life presents.

As for the Goddess, she doesn't know either. If you examine this carefully, you will see she is just a puppet on a string. Every teacher is a puppet on a string, going through antics to teach what is essentially unteachable—because every one of us already has it. Every teacher must make a fool out of himself or herself, saying things that are unnecessary because the teacher is already talking to a Buddha, to a complete and perfect being. This is the realm where yin and yang do not exist. How could the Goddess know? She said that she searched for her female state for twelve years and didn't find it. You need a reference system to find it. She is totally intimate with herself. To be totally intimate means to contain everything. The reference system is gone. When you become the barrier, there is nothing to compare it to. The barrier is gone. When you become Mu, the whole universe is Mu. There is nothing to compare it to. The reference system is gone.

Ever the same, / The moon among the clouds, / Different from each other, / The mountain and the valley. / Isn't it wonderful? / Isn't it miraculous? / Is this one, or is it two? On one side is the absolute: no eye, ear, nose, tongue, body, mind, no color, sound, taste, touch, phenomenon. There is neither holy nor profane, neither male nor female. The absolute basis of reality. On the other side is eye, ear, nose, tongue, body, mind, color, sound, smell, taste, touch, phenomenon. There is a reference system. There is good and there is evil. There is male and there is female. There is up and there is down. There is holy and there is profane. The truth of the Buddhadharma can be found in neither of these extremes. "The truth of the Buddhadharma cannot be found in speech, nor can it be found in silence." Then what is it? Beyond the absolute, beyond the relative, beyond male and female—what is the truth? What is reality? What is life? Who are you? The Goddess doesn't know. Very intimate, very intimate indeed. Shariputra doesn't know. So where do you find yourself? If all things do not exist, then what is real and what is reality? What does the Goddess mean that there are no men and women in reality? What does the Buddha mean by "in things there is neither male nor female"? What does the Goddess mean by "there is perfect enlightenment because there is no attainment of perfect enlightenment"? Don't tell me—show me!

THERE IS NEITHER HOLY NOR PROFANE, NEITHER MALE NOR FEMALE

I have always been struck by the fact that in Buddhist literature the only reference to women is usually the old woman on the roadside who is enlightened but has no identity. Somehow, this is what we have inherited, this partial history of Zen. But I know in my bones that there is more to it than that. Whatever happened to the nun Myozen, who enlightened seventeen monks, who was a successor of Gyozan? Why don't we have something in the literature about her? Whatever happened to Master Isan's successor Iron Grindstone Liu? She was called "Iron Grindstone" because she would devour people like a lion in Dharma Combat. Surely, there must be some record of her. Why didn't it come down to us? I think the reason is that the historians have been men, and that is what has been passed on from China to Japan to America. Even today, when you find out who the translators are and who the Buddhist historians are, you find out that they are still almost entirely men. And that means that everything that we are doing and all the women successors who are emerging are going to have the same fate as their predecessors, until more women become historians. The same thing is true in the black movement. There was no black history forty years ago. Black history suddenly happened because black historians happened. The information is there somewhere, but history is written according to the prejudice of the historians. In order to find out more about these people who seem to have disappeared, women have to enter the ranks of Buddhist scholasticism. Empress Wu reigned in the Golden Age of Zen in China, and I'm sure during that period of time there were many, many great female teachers and lineages of women. Where did they disappear to? Who are they? What were their teachings? Where are the collected teachings of those women? There are two English translations of the *Vimalakirti Sutra* available, both of them by men. One is a bit more liberated than the other, and the differences in the language are enormous.

THERE WERE MANY GREAT FEMALE TEACHERS AND LINEAGES OF WOMEN.

The past has already happened and the future hasn't happened yet. What is right here right now? Where do you find yourself? Indeed, what is the self? Maleness? Femaleness? Student, teacher, parent, child, good, bad, happy, sad, young, old, lover, hater? Who are you? If you can speak a word on this, then you will know that the meeting at the house of Vimalakirti is definitely present here.

10

"LIKE A DREAM"

Blue Cliff Record: Case 40

MASTER ENGO'S POINTER

WHEN THE ACTION of the mind has stopped and is swept away, the iron tree will bloom. Can you show it? Even a crafty person will become a cropper here. Even if you excel in every way, you will still have your nostrils pierced. Where are the complications? Listen to the following:

MAIN CASE

Rikyu Taifu said to Nansen, "Johoshi has said the heaven and earth and I are of the same root. All things and I are of one substance. Isn't that fantastic!" Nansen pointed to a flower in the garden, called Taifu to him, and said, "People these days see this flower as though they were in a dream."

MASTER SETCHO'S VERSE

Hearing, seeing, touching, and knowing
　　are not one and one.
Mountains and rivers
　　should not be viewed in the mirror.
The frosty sky, the setting moon at midnight—
With whom will the serene waters of the lake
　　reflect the shadows, cold, in a clear pool?

The koans of *The Blue Cliff Record* use a great deal of metaphor and poetry to clarify points of the dharma. Poetry (as well as art in general) has always been a part of the history of religion. Art and religion have long been connected in one way or another—every religion of the world has its sacred arts. Usually, however, the sacred arts are involved with icons, with worship, with recording the words or the mystical experience of the particular religion's founder. Zen art functions in a very different way.

IN ZEN, ART CAN BECOME IN ITSELF A DIRECT POINTING TO THE MIND.

The art can become in itself a direct pointing to the mind, as in the case of the poetry and metaphor of this koan. To see a koan is to be the koan, and to be the koan—or *any* barrier—means to forget the self, to let go of the idea of a separate self, the idea that the bag of skin is who we are. Sometimes even the images that great masters like Sengai and Hakuin painted and gave to their students had a way of directly pointing to the mind. It is that direct pointing to the mind that is the teaching of Zen.

Everything else is decoration. In this practice, it is necessary for each one of us to have the same realization as that of the Buddha. The mystical experience of the Buddha is not to be understood, imitated, or believed, but to be intimately and directly experienced. Here at Doshinji, art is one of the seven areas of Zen training. A student trains not only in zazen, Zen study (face-to-face teaching and koans), academic study (study of the sutras), liturgy, body practice, and work practice, but in art as well. It is important to understand that Zen art is not "art," because only then can you begin to understand "art." When *you* create art, you create a self. When *art* creates art, the self forgets the self. To forget the self is to be really intimate with the self. To really be intimate with the self is to be intimate with "the ten thousand things"; that is, with the whole phenomenal universe. Dogen said, "Seeing form with the whole body and mind, hearing sound with the whole body and mind, one understands them intimately." Isn't this "art creating art"? Isn't it the brush painting by itself? Music, but no musician? The dance, but no dancer to be found? "To see forms intimately is to see with the ear, hear with the eye. To hear sounds intimately is to hear with the eye and see with the ear. The eye hearing and the ear seeing is the self really being intimate with the self."

In his pointer, Master Engo says: *When the action of the mind has stopped and is swept away, the iron tree will bloom.* We are constantly involved with mental activity, and that mental activity constantly separates us from what we're doing. We're always preoccupied with something, and usually it has to do with something not happening at the moment. We're preoccupied with the past, yet it doesn't exist; it's already happened. Or we're preoccupied with the future, yet it, too, doesn't exist; it hasn't happened yet. While we involve ourselves with past and future, we miss the moment-to-moment awareness of our life.

When the action of the mind has stopped and is swept away, the stone woman will give birth to a child in the middle of the night. All kinds of miraculous things take place. Engo says: *Even a crafty person will become a cropper here.* That means that you can act as though you understand, you can even believe it, but unless it's your own being, your own experience, you have separated yourself from it. This is the point of the koan, of what is going on with Rikyu Taifu. It's all up in his head, even though he has already had a deep opening experience with Master Nansen. That's why Engo says, "Can you show it? Without opening your mouth, can you show it?" Sure, heaven and earth are one, you and I are the same thing—but to talk about it is one thing, to show it is another. You and I are the same thing, yet I am not you and you are not me. Where do you put that to rest? *Heaven and earth and I are of the same root. All things and I are of one substance.* Still, Nansen "pierced his nostrils." That means Nansen took him like a bull with a nose ring and led him around. He's not free; he's caught up in the words and ideas that describe reality, and is missing the

YOU AND I ARE THE SAME THING, YET I AM NOT YOU AND YOU ARE NOT ME.

95

reality itself. The minute he opens his mouth, he reveals his point of attachment.

Where are the complications? Rikyu Taifu said: *Heaven and earth and I are of the same root. All things and I are of one substance. Isn't that fantastic!* Nansen pointed to a peony in the garden, called Taifu, and said: *People these days look at this flower as though they were in a dream.* Nansen was Joshu's teacher and one of the great masters during the T'ang dynasty. He was probably one of the greatest successors of Master Baso. One day Baso, who had eighty-four enlightened successors, said: "The sutras are in the hands of Seido [one of his successors], Zen is in the hands of Hyakujo [another of his great successors], but only Nansen surpasses the world of things." This koan is taking place in the later years of Nansen's teaching, when he was very ripe. Taifu was a very high government official and one of Nansen's students. He was, to give an example, the equivalent of a member of the U.S. Supreme Court. In one dialogue with Nansen, Taifu said, "I've raised a goose in a bottle, and it gradually grew too big to get out without breaking the bottle or injuring the goose. How would you get it out?" Nansen said, "Taifu!" Taifu said, "Yes?" Nansen said, "It's out!" At that, Taifu was awakened. What did Taifu see? What is it that he realized? What was it that the turning word of Nansen was able to do for him?

Taifu was a student of the discourses of Master Jo, a fifth-century scholar. Taifu loved to study the works of Jo, and during a walk with Nansen, he quoted two lines from one of Jo's discourses: "Heaven and earth and I are of the same root. The ten thousand things and I are one body." Then he commented, "Isn't Dharma Master Jo wonderful!" Taifu's first opening came in that mondo with Nansen about the goose, and this quotation from the discourse of Jo shows the merging of subject and object, the revealing of the nature of things, the showing of no separation. "To study the Buddha Way is to study the self. To study the self is to forget the self. To forget the self is to be enlightened by the ten thousand things." When you forget the self, what you let go of is the only thing that separates you from everything else. It is the same thing whether we're talking about a work of art, the entire universe, breakfast, or a relationship. The only thing that separates you is the idea that you are separated. The bag of skin. We think everything inside the bag of skin is "me" and everything outside is "other." It is not like that at all. When we realize that there is no inside or outside, that the skin bag is not a barrier, that a separate self is an idea, an illusion, then the self is forgotten and the ten thousand things return to the self, where they've always been—where they are *right now*.

What is it that remains when the self is forgotten? To forget the self is a scary thing, even though the fact is that there isn't any self and we've just created the idea that it exists. What remains when the self is forgotten? *Everything.* The whole universe remains, but there is no longer a barrier between you and it. Past, present, and future—the entirety of the ten thousand things—is what remains. But talking about it doesn't reach it. It must be realized directly. WHAT REMAINS WHEN THE SELF IS FORGOTTEN?

Taifu's comment on Jo's discourse is what we call "stinky." It is "stinky" or "clinging" Zen because Taifu was clinging to his experience of enlightenment. His comment has the "smell" of Zen about it, and to that extent he is green. Remember, it doesn't matter what you attach to; whether it's delusion or enlightenment, attachment is attachment. Whether it is a beautiful new Mercedes or Buddhism that you attach to, it is still attachment. And in order to attach you need a separate self and something to attach to: that is the delusion. Delusion is a sickness, but enlightenment, too, can be a sickness. It's called "the sickness of having no sickness." *Anything* we attach to becomes a disease.

Nansen, in deep compassion, points out the sickness for Taifu. Pointing to a flower in the garden, he says: *People these days see this flower as if they were in a dream.* In the closing lines of *The Diamond Sutra,* the Buddha says, "Thus shall you think of all this fleeting world; / A star at dawn, a bubble in a stream; / A flash of lightning in a summer cloud / A flickering lamp, a phantom, and a dream." The reality that happens in a dream and the one that happens in the world are equally real. That is what is meant when we say: "What you do and what happens to you are the same thing." That's why it's impossible to avoid taking responsibility for our life once we realize that we create it. We create the delusion, the enlightenment, the pain, and we can create the joy. We can create neither enlightenment nor delusion, neither pain nor joy. What is that like? What is it that falls in neither extreme? What is it that is neither absolute nor relative? If we realize the dream of this moment, then you and I and everything in the universe are a dream, and there is nothing outside of "dream." There is nothing to compare it with; therefore, it is the same as saying, "There is no dream at all." Do you understand?

WHAT YOU DO AND WHAT HAP-PENS TO YOU ARE THE SAME THING.

Nansen doesn't say, "It is a dream." He says, *People these days see this flower as if they were in a dream.* It's not called "a dream"; it's not called "not-a-dream." Nor is it called "neither a dream nor not-a-dream." What is it? Master Dogen says, "The holding up of the flower by the Buddha and Mahakashyapa's smile is explaining a dream within a dream. And the second ancestor's [Eka's] prostration and attaining the marrow is also explaining a dream within a dream." He is speaking of the mind-to-mind transmission of the dharma from the Buddha to his first disciple, and from the first ancestor of Zen to his first disciple. Is that what practice is? If everything is a dream, then what is real? What is reality? And what about Taifu in this koan—what is his understanding? What is the common root of heaven and earth? What is the common body of the ten thousand things? *People see this flower as if they were in a dream.* The pure perception of seeing, before we step back from it, is pure cognition. Then, within an instant, we separate ourselves. When you touch something, the moment of touch is pure. No self. A second later, the self and the thing being touched become two. This is the difference between looking and seeing. Seeing is deep; the whole body and mind are involved. In looking there are always two: the person and the thing seen.

SEEING IS DEEP: THE WHOLE BODY AND MIND ARE INVOLVED.

MASTER SETCHO'S VERSE

Hearing, seeing, touching, and knowing
  are not one and one.
Mountains and rivers
  should not be viewed in a mirror.
The frosty sky, the setting moon at midnight—
With whom will the serene waters of the lake
  reflect the shadows, cold, in a clear pool?

Although there are spirits and humans, sages and ordinary people, each is distinct, yet all have one nature and one substance. An ancient master said, "Heaven and earth, the whole world, is just one self. When cold, it is cold throughout heaven and earth. When hot, it is hot throughout heaven and earth. When it exists, all throughout heaven and earth exists. When it does not exist, heaven and earth do not exist. When affirmed, all throughout heaven and earth, *is*. When denied, all throughout heaven and earth, *is not*." Do you understand the words of that ancient master? Another master said of the same subject, "He, he, he, she, she, she, I, I, I, south, north, east, west—everything is all right. All right or not all right, only for me, there is nothing not all right." That is the point of the quotation. Tell me, what root do the ten thousand things share? Which body do they have in common?

WHAT ROOT DO THE TEN THOUSAND THINGS SHARE?

Hearing, seeing, touching, and knowing are not one and one. The phrase "not one and one" means not two, not separate, not distinct from each other. Sensation and cognition are not separate from each other. *Mountains and rivers should not be viewed in a mirror.* If you say they are seen in a

99

mirror, then they are apart from where the mirror is. Mountains and rivers, the great earth, plants, trees, and forest—don't use a mirror to see them. Don't separate yourself. Just let mountains be mountains and rivers be rivers. Each thing abides in its normal state. *Mountains and rivers are not viewed in a mirror.* Tell me, where can you see them? Do you understand? If you can get that far, then the thing is to turn toward the next line: *The frosty sky, the setting moon at midnight— / With whom will the serene waters of the lake reflect the shadows, cold, in a clear pool?* Do you think that in his verse Setcho is reflecting himself? Or is he reflecting together with everyone? Or reflecting with no one? It is necessary to cut off all mental activities and understanding before you can reach the place Setcho is coming from. Where was Taifu's fault? Where was he lacking? What about the old, ripe plum, Master Nansen—where does he abide? What does he hold on to? "High in these mountains there is an old pond / Deep or shallow, its bottom has never been seen."

With whom will the serene waters of the lake reflect the shadows, cold, in a clear pool? Right now, we don't need a clear pool. And we don't have to wait for the moon to set in the frosty sky. Right now, how is it? Right now, where is your practice? Where do you find yourself? That is all there is—this right now. Don't miss it. It is your life.

EACH THING ABIDES IN ITS NORMAL STATE.

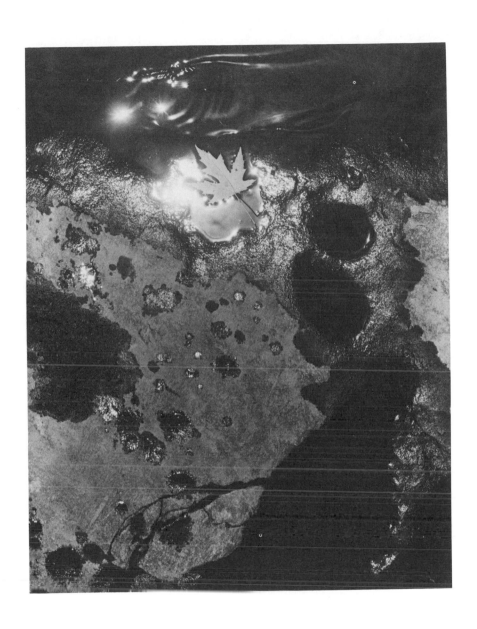

11

ACCOMPLISHING BUDDHA'S GREAT WISDOM

T HE GREAT MASTER DOGEN taught that there are four prajnas: suffering, the cause of suffering, the extinguishing of suffering, and the path. And also that there are six prajnas: giving, precepts, patience, effort, contemplation, and wisdom. Moreover, there is one prajna paramita: Anuttara-samyak-sambodhi (the incomparable, unsurpassable Way), which is actualized in this very moment.

Prajna is usually translated as "wisdom." This seems the closest word to it that we have in the English language, even though it is a kind of misleading application of the term. Ordinarily, when we think of wisdom, we think of accumulated philosophical or scientific knowledge, or of a wise attitude or action. But "accumulated" implies a sense of gathering. Gathering from where? Prajna is itself the realization of no separation, of no inside or outside. By its very definition "knowledge" is dualistic; it separates the "knower" from the thing that the knower "knows." The word *prajna* in Buddhism means much more than accumulated data, much more than understanding or even believing. It has to do with a direct and intimate experience of our very life itself. Prajna is not something we "get." It has never been attained. Even Buddha himself did not attain it! It does not come from the outside. It cannot be given, and it cannot be received. Where does it come from? It does not come; it does not go. What is it? Where is it?

The great Master Dogen says in this paragraph that prajna is suffering *(dukkha)*, the first of the Four Noble Truths of Buddhism. A more precise way of saying it is that prajna is the truth of suffering. Implicit in it is the cause of suffering; within suffering itself is its source. Also, within the cause of suffering is the seed of the cessation of suffering, and implicit in the cessation of suffering is the path or means to its cessation. In a sense, then, this first of the Four Noble Truths contains each of the other three.

Many people think of Buddhism as being very pessimistic because of this principal Noble Truth, "Life is suffering." It was the beginning of the Buddha's teaching, the first turning of the Dharma Wheel. But Buddhism is neither pessimistic nor optimistic; if anything, it is simply realistic. It takes a realistic view of life and the world, and doesn't lull us into living in a fool's paradise. It doesn't frighten us with imaginary fears nor agonize us with guilt for all kinds of sins, but tells us exactly what we are and what the world is. The Pali word *dukkha* in ordinary usage means "suffering," "pain," "sorrow," or "misery," and contrasts with the Pali term for "happiness," "comfort," or "ease." But *dukkha* not only indicates this ordinary meaning, but also includes deeper ideas such as imperfection, emptiness, unsubstantiality.

It includes, for instance, what we normally call "happiness"—ordinary happiness, spiritual happiness, both the happiness of family life and that of a recluse, of sense pleasures and renunciation, of attachment and detachment, physical happiness and mental happiness. All of these are included in dukkha. Even the very pure spiritual states of *dhyana* attained by the practice of higher meditation, free from even a shadow of suffering in the accepted sense of the word, is part of this dukkha. Whatever is impermanent is, by its very nature, dukkha.

Master Dogen taught that prajna is the truth of the

cause of suffering. The cause of suffering is thirst, desire, greed, craving, or attachment to sense pleasures, wealth, power, ideas, ideal views, opinions, theories, or conceptions. All of these beliefs spring from the same place—the idea that the self is a separate entity, distinct from the rest of the universe, that who we are is this bag of skin, and that everything inside it is "me" and everything outside it is the rest of the universe. The moment we start from that premise, all our delusion, confusion, and suffering necessarily follow. What this skin bag is, is an idea. It is a way of using your mind. When you really look at who you are, what your life is, what this universe is, and peel back the conditioning of your parents, teachers, peers, education, nation, culture, everything that reinforces the idea of separation, when you get beneath all of that to the ground of being, you realize that this bag of skin is just a small part of what you really are.

Master Dogen taught that prajna is not only the truth of suffering and the truth of the cause of suffering, but also the truth of the extinguishing of suffering, *nirodha*. To eliminate dukkha completely, one has to eliminate the root of it, which is thirst. We have to extinguish thirst. He also taught that prajna is the truth of the path (*magga*). This is generally referred to as the Eightfold Path of the Buddha and consists of eight categories: right understanding, right thought, right speech, right action, right livelihood, right effort, right mindfulness, and right concentration. In a sense, practically the whole teaching of the Buddha, the teaching he was devoted to for forty-five years, all deals in one way or another with this Eightfold Path. He explained it in different ways, with different words to different people according to the stage of their development and capacity to understand and follow him, but the essence of the thousands of discourses and sutras in Buddhist scriptures is to be found in this Noble Eightfold Path.

Although the word *right* is generally used in translations of the eight categories of the path, it might be better un-

WE HAVE TO
EXTINGUISH
THIRST.

derstood if the word *perfect* or *absolute* was used instead. We could read "right understanding," then, as perfect or absolute understanding, and so on—absolute thought, absolute speech, absolute action, absolute livelihood, absolute effort, absolute mindfulness, and absolute concentration. Two key aspects of the Buddhist teachings are wisdom and compassion. Wisdom is the realization of the nature of the self, the direct experience of having forgotten the self and being enlightened by the ten thousand things. When this wisdom is realized directly and intimately, it gives rise to compassion, the manifestation of wisdom in action. Wisdom and compassion are two parts of the same reality. Compassion functions with no sense of separation, no sense of subject-object duality. It happens the way you grow your hair: with no effort. Absolute understanding and absolute thought in the Eightfold Path are this wisdom. Absolute speech, action and livelihood are the activity of wisdom in the world; they are compassion, the manifesting of the ethical teachings of the Buddha. Absolute effort, mindfulness, and concentration are the mental disciplines, the consequences of wisdom and compassion.

WISDOM AND COMPASSION ARE TWO PARTS OF THE SAME REALITY.

The great Master Dogen also taught that there are six prajnas: the prajna of giving, the prajna of the precepts, the prajna of patience, the prajna of effort, the prajna of contemplation, and the prajna of wisdom. These prajnas are the six actions of the bodhisattva, also called the six paramitas.

Paramita is the other shore. Prajna paramita is the wisdom of the other shore, the crossing over from delusion to enlightenment. In *The Heart Sutra* we chant that all dharmas are formed of emptiness, are neither born nor destroyed, neither stained nor pure, without loss and gain. "Form is no other than emptiness; emptiness no other than form. Form is exactly emptiness and emptiness exactly form." The phenomenal world *is* the absolute. The absolute *is* the phenomenal; they are not two, not separate. This shore and the other shore are not two, not separate.

Whether we realize it or not, there is no separation to begin with. This is why there is no gain and no loss. We only place "it" outside ourselves by the way we use our minds. The fact is that it is not outside ourselves, and can't be found "out there." When we are looking and searching and grasping, we miss it. That is why we say that our practice is always right here, right now, right where we sit. That is where the delusion is created, and where it is finally going to be put to rest. Only you can do it; no one can do it for you. The Buddha himself couldn't do it for you.

All the teaching of the Buddha comes from the same place—no-self. When you realize no-self, there can't be any separation. That's what Master Dogen is talking about when he says: "To study the Buddha Way is to study the self. To study the self is to forget the self. To forget the self is to be enlightened by the ten thousand things. To be enlightened by the ten thousand things is to cast off body and mind of self and other." Once the self is forgotten, the barrier that separates us from the rest of the universe is gone. Then it makes sense: no gain, no loss, no coming, no going. It's all complete right where you are. When you look from that perspective at *dana* paramita, the paramita of giving, there is no giver and no receiver, nothing to give and nothing to receive. The same thing is functioning in compassion, the manifestation of wisdom in action. *Sila*, the Buddhist precepts, are also based on no-self. In a sense, what the precepts are is a definition of the life of a Buddha. In the beginning of our practice we take the precepts as an act of faith, but before our training is completed, they must be a manifestation of our life. They must be realized and actualized as a manifestation "in the world" of no-self. In fact, they are the activity of the world itself. The same thing is operating with the paramitas of patience, effort, and dhyana.

All of these pieces are one prajna paramita, one "wisdom of the other shore," which is anuttara-samyak-sambodhi, the incomparable, unsurpassable way actual-

"TO STUDY THE SELF IS TO FORGET THE SELF."

ized in this very moment. This is the meaning of "Practice and enlightenment are one," the heart of Master Dogen's teaching. When you are practicing, you are manifesting the life of the Buddha. You are manifesting supreme enlightenment; the goal and the process are not two separate things. What does this mean in terms of our life, in terms of our practice? *The Heart Sutra* says that the bodhisattva lives prajna paramita, lives the wisdom of the other shore. "With no hindrance in the mind; no hindrance, therefore, no fear." Where does the hindrance come from? Where do the barriers arise from? When a barrier comes up, we say, "Be the barrier." What you do when you become the barrier is acknowledge the reality of who you are. To become the barrier is to return things to the way they are. "It" is not something outside of you. The "hindrance" is yourself. One of the beautiful things that happens in this practice is the unavoidable realization of responsibility. The realization that what you do and what happens to you are the same thing. You are totally responsible for everything, for the whole catastrophe. This is kind of overwhelming, in a sense, but at the same time it is incredibly freeing and liberating because you can no longer kid yourself into being a victim. You are responsible; you can no longer blame. It no longer makes any sense to say, "It's his fault; he made me angry." How could "he" make you angry? Only you can make you angry. You realize that you are in charge, that there is something you can do about it. You're not helpless, and you don't have to sit around waiting for good luck. How you live your life, how you practice, determines what you experience in your life. It has nothing to do with good or bad, nothing to do with circumstances.

YOU ARE RE-SPONSIBLE FOR THE WHOLE CA-TASTROPHE.

"All past, present, and future Buddhas live prajna paramita and therefore obtain anuttara-samyak-sambodhi." To live it means to practice it from moment-to-moment. To practice what? Prajna paramita, the wisdom of the other shore. Where is the other shore? You should look right where you sit. In practice, the self asserts itself in all kinds of ways: pain, boredom, anxiety, fear, anger. That is the material that practice is made of. When you hurt, you know why you are hurting: you're sitting cross-legged for a long period of time. If you were sitting on a bus for ten hours, your behind and your legs would hurt. Somehow, though, when that pain comes up in sitting, we have to find something else to blame it on. What happens is that all the anger we've hidden in corners and suppressed begins to manifest itself. We find someone to blame, something to get angry at. Not everybody gets angry, however; some students manifest their pain as fear and become frightened by it. Some manifest it by withdrawing, retreating. All of this is part of getting to the bottom of this great matter. You begin to see that the pain, anger, fear, and greed is what makes the illusion of self exist. It's just like all the many things we attach to: my life, my car, my house, my garden, my dog, my cat, my ideas, my opinions, my this, my that. I must exist, since I have all these things. Fear and anger function in the same way.

We need to deal with the baggage, to really see how the illusion of self arises and get beyond pulling back from it. The more we pull back, the bigger the illusion becomes. Only when we go into it, when we become the barrier, become the cause, become the breath, become prajna paramita and stop separating ourselves will that other shore (which is nothing but this shore) become obvious.

So what will you do? How will you do it? When will you do it? Will you do it tomorrow? Tomorrow doesn't exist; it hasn't happened yet. Yesterday doesn't exist; it has already happened. What is here right now? That is the point of entry. Even to say "entry" is extra because there is no place to enter. There is no inside or outside. See what it is that sits on your *zafu.* Your practice and your life are always right here, right now. See it now and give life to the Buddha. See it right now and really be intimate with yourself. This is "to accomplish Buddha's Great Wisdom."

WHAT IS HERE RIGHT NOW? THAT IS THE POINT OF ENTRY.

12

TRANSMISSION OF THE LIGHT

FROM ITS EARLIEST BEGINNINGS, the uniqueness of the life of Zen has been the fact of the religious experience personally attained by each individual. From the beginning, initiation that followed any ritual or scripture was utterly denied in Zen. Zen transmission is always based on the actual experience of each individual; and at the same time, the experience of the individual and that of the teacher are to be one and the same. This is the reason that Zen, while insisting on the absolute necessity of standing on one's own personal, direct experience, attaches great importance to the teacher-disciple transmission and takes it very seriously. If this is neglected, the life of the true, live Zen tradition will immediately be extinguished. This teacher-disciple transmission is called the Transmission of the Light, or the Transmission of the Lamp. The "light" mentioned is enlightenment. When we use the word *ignorance* in Buddhism, it literally means "having no light" or "not knowing what is real." Enlightenment means "having light" and "seeing what is real." When the first thought is deluded, all subsequent thoughts are deluded. When the first thought springs from enlightenment, all subsequent thoughts are enlightened. The uniqueness of our practice, for which the Transmission of the Light serves as testimony, lies in the fact that it is a direct, mind-to-mind transmission. Christianity, Judaism, Hinduism, and Islam, to mention just a few religious forms, are all

ZEN IS BASED ON PERSONAL, DIRECT EXPERIENCE.

based primarily on a mystical experience of some sort that the founders originally had. After a while, that mystical experience becomes part of a record, written in the scriptures, and part of the rituals, laws, commandments, and moral precepts. What the followers or disciples do is repeat, read, and recite these ideas and concepts, talk to each other about them, study them, intellectualize and philosophize about them. They are not, however, required to experience them directly. If you want to be a teacher of Christianity, you get a doctorate in theology. You go to school for a number of years and pass examinations and write a dissertation. There is no requirement that you experience the way of Christ, that you personally experience the realization of Christ. Much of Buddhism is the same way, but in Zen the practice is different. Zen is a "special transmission, outside the scriptures, with no dependence on words and letters." It is "a direct pointing at the human mind and the attainment of Buddhahood." Only *that* is the transmission of the light.

What, then, is this "direct pointing at the human mind and the attainment of Buddhahood"?

Ananda asked Mahakashyapa, "When the World-Honored One gave you the *kesa* [robe] of golden cloth, did he give you anything else?"

Kashyapa said, "Ananda!"

Ananda said, "Yes, Master!"

Kashyapa said, "Take down the flagpole at the gate."

This is the whole universe calling out and the ten thousand dharmas answering. Like two mirrors reflecting each other, the "eternal spring is not subject to climate or season." This is the moment and place that transcends time and space. If you can penetrate to the truth of this calling out and answering, you will see into Zen's "family shame" and take down not only the flagpole, but Kashyapa, and this great mountain as well. This is the ancestral light being transmitted from generation to generation.

THIS IS THE LIGHT TRANSMITTED FROM GENERATION TO GENERATION.

This koan is an account of the transmission of the dharma from Mahakashyapa, who had received it from Shakyamuni Buddha, to Ananda, the second ancestor of our lineage. Ananda, whose name means "happiness and joy," was actually the cousin of Shakyamuni Buddha. Said to be very brilliant, he was born on the night that Shakyamuni Buddha attained enlightenment, December 8. He was the *jisha*, or attendant, to the Buddha for twenty years. For those twenty years, every place the Buddha went, Ananda was there. Every talk that the Buddha gave, from the time he joined him until the Buddha's death, Ananda heard. Not only did he hear the talks, but because he had an incredible, photographic memory, he remembered them word for word. He was there when Shakyamuni Buddha transmitted the dharma to Mahakashyapa, one of the thousands of people in the assembly when Buddha held up the flower. Along with the thousands of other people, he didn't get it.

EVERY TALK THAT THE BUDDHA GAVE, ANANDA HEARD.

It is said that Ananda was "foremost in learning." The Buddha himself gave him approval many times, but never transmitted to him. He actually said to Ananda after he transmitted to Kashyapa, "Help to communicate the teaching." As a result of that, Ananda became Kashyapa's attendant for another twenty years after the Buddha died, following him around and listening to all the discourses he gave on the teaching. He heard everything there was to hear about this teaching—forty years of hearing. Once he was called into an assembly of the disciples and was asked to recite the Buddha's teaching. Hearing him, the disciples said, "It is like a cup of water being poured into another cup without spilling any." Kashyapa said to Ananda, "Everyone is looking to you to please ascend the seat and recite the sayings of the Buddha." Ananda, accepting Kashyapa's request, rose and bowed to the assembly, ascended the high seat, and recounted, "Thus did I hear one time when the Buddha was in . . ." in the way all the sutras start. He commenced reciting all of the Buddha's teachings, which formed the basis of all the written records to follow. When he had finished, Kashyapa said to the disciples, "Is this any different than what the Buddha taught?" and the disciples confirmed that it was no different. The disciples were all great practitioners; they did not forget anything they heard. In complete agreement they said, "Is the realized one repeating himself? Is this Ananda talking? The waters of the ocean of the Buddha's teaching have flowed into Ananda." All of the teachings of the Buddha that have come down to the present are those spoken by Ananda. It is obvious from this that the Way doesn't depend upon great learning. Ananda followed Kashyapa for twenty years, but his realization of enlightenment finally came as indicated in the main case of this koan. Ananda was deeply fond of learning. Master Keizan said, "This is why he had not truly realized enlightenment. Shakyamuni practiced vigorously, and therefore he attained enlightenment. Surely, much learning is a hindrance on the Way. This is proof of that." This is why the *Avatamsaka Sutra* says, "Much learning is like a poor man counting another's treasures, without a half-cent of his own."

Ananda, filled with this great learning, obviously must have felt there was something he was missing, or else why would the Buddha have transmitted to Kashyapa and not to him? One day he said to Kashyapa, "On Mount Gudhakutra when the Buddha transmitted the golden kesa to you, did he give you anything else?" Forty years after witnessing the transmission, he wanted to know if anything else was transmitted. Being a good teacher, Kashyapa answered him. When a question is asked, there is no way a teacher will avoid answering it. It must be answered. Always, the question is answered. Always. "Was anything else transmitted?" Kashyapa said, "Ananda!" Ananda said, "Yes, Master!" "Take down the flagpole." And at that, Ananda was enlightened.

WHEN A
QUESTION IS
ASKED, THE
TEACHER
MUST AN-
SWER IT.

Intellectual understanding is obviously important. But to have intellectual understanding without realization is "to have the eyes closed in broad daylight." To have realization without intellectual understanding is "to have the eyes open in darkness." To have both intellectual understanding and realization is "to have the eyes open in the bright light of day." They both are necessary. To understand something intellectually and not have personally realized it just doesn't cut it. Imagine yourself wanting to cross a thousand miles of treacherous mountains and jungles. Nobody has ever done it before, but you want to do it. You need a guide and are presented two possibilities, one is a person with a doctorate from Harvard in map-reading, mountaineering, and traversing jungles. The other is an illiterate with no formal education, a native who has been living in the jungle for twenty years. Which one are you going to go with? The one with experience, or the one who has learned it from a book? Obviously, the experience is important. Obviously, both are even better.

The incredible thing that has happened in just the twenty-some years that formal Zen training has been accessible in America is that less than a dozen of the nearly two hundred second- and third-generation teachers here in the West have received the authentic transmission. Perhaps only a handful of that dozen have completed the rigorous training that is characteristic of Master Rinzai, Master Dogen, Joshu, or Unmon. Already in this short period of time an entire generation of self-appointed, self-styled gurus eager to Westernize Buddhism are taking the life and spirit out of it by trying to package it for the supermarket. There is a rich religious and mystical tradition based upon direct personal experience that is a vital part of Zen training. So much of that is being lost in the West. It is like the blind leading the blind. I remember something my grandmother used to say, commenting on my relationship to money, when I was a child. She only spoke Italian, and in Italian, it had the flavor of a poem. The poem said something like, "Money in your hands is like a lantern in the hands of a blind man." Isn't it the same here? The purported transmission of the light from inau-

TO HAVE BOTH UNDERSTANDING AND REALIZATION IS "TO HAVE THE EYES OPEN IN THE BRIGHT LIGHT OF DAY."

115

thentic teachers is like the light going from one blind person to another.

Ananda asked, "When the World-Honored One gave you the golden kesa, did he give you anything else?" Mahakashyapa answered him. "Ananda!" Ananda answered back, "Yes, Master!" What did Ananda see? "The whole universe called out; the ten thousand dharmas answered." The "whole universe" and the "ten thousand dharmas" are different names for the same thing. "Like two mirrors reflecting each other, the eternal spring is not subject to climate or season. This is the moment and the place that transcends time and space." That was the complete identification between teacher and disciple. But teachers always call out to disciples:

"Jisha!"

"Yes!"

Why doesn't enlightenment happen? What was so special about this calling and answering? What did Ananda see? Kashyapa says, "Take down the flagpole," and at that moment, Ananda is enlightened. The flagpole was used to hoist a flag whenever a *teisho* (sermon) was being given. When the flag was up, the teaching was being expounded. When the flag was down, the teaching was completed. Basically, then, Kashyapa was approving Ananda. "Ananda!" "Yes, Master!" "Take down the flagpole!" The lecture is concluded, the teaching has been completed. But there is something more going on. This has been an explanation—what does it mean in terms of the live truth? You, right now on this mountain, how do you take down the flagpole?

Ananda went to the description of reality, the words and explanations, the sutras, the scriptures, the thousands of discourses—all that he had stored away like a human computer, though he didn't really get it. Twenty years he studied with the Buddha, and then he continued with Mayakashyapa for twenty years more. Finally, it dawned on him that something was going on, that this Kashyapa

"TAKE DOWN THE FLAGPOLE!"

must have gotten something other than the brocade robe. In fact, Master Keizan speaks of it in his discourse on the koan:

> As for the present incident, Ananda had thought that Kashyapa received the golden vestment and was a disciple of the Buddha, but other than that there was nothing special. Nevertheless, after following Kashyapa and attending him closely, he thought Kashyapa had realized something more. Kashyapa then knew that the time was ripe and called out to him. Like a valley spirit echoing in response to a call, like a spark issuing from a stone, Ananda immediately responded. "Ananda!" "Yes, Master!" "Take down the flagpole!" If you want to find out what this Way really is, do not be fond of great learning; just be vigorous in your spiritual practice. Yet, I dare say that there must be something besides the handing on of the robe. Thus, once he said, "Elder brother and teacher, the World-Honored One bequeathed the golden robe to you; what else did he transmit?" Kashyapa, realizing the time was ripe, called, "Ananda!" Ananda responded. Kashyapa said back, "Take down the banner pole from the gate." Ananda was greatly enlightened as he heard this. The Buddha's robe spontaneously entered Ananda's head.

The "ripeness" Keizan speaks of is the key. When you look at the enlightenment experiences of these various ancestors, you see that all sorts of things functioned as triggering mechanisms for the realization of enlightenment. For example, Shakyamuni Buddha sat under the bodhi tree doing zazen, saw the morning star, and experienced great enlightenment, anuttara-samyak-sambodhi. Without understanding what was going on, you might think that the bodhi tree was responsible and that we should all get ourselves a special tree to sit under in order to get enlightened. Or you might sit around waiting for the morning star, figuring that is it. Look at Mahakashyapa—Buddha held up a flower and blinked his eyes, Kashyapa smiled,

"RIPENESS" IS THE KEY.

and the transmission was complete. Was it the smile? The flower? The blinking of the eyes? We could have a whole religious sect that blinks eyes and holds up flowers. How about Ananda with the calling out and answering, the taking down of the flagpole? Or the instance of a pebble striking bamboo? One of the masters got his leg caught in a door. He went to call on his teacher, knocked on the door, the teacher opened it, and just as the student was about to speak, the teacher slammed the door in his face. The student went back into the zendo and sat zazen with his burning question. Again he went to the teacher's cottage and knocked on the door. The teacher opened the door and said, "Oh, you," and slammed it again. He went back and sat some more, determined to get in to see the teacher. He went back again, knocked on the door, and when the teacher opened it, he shoved his foot into the doorway. The teacher slammed the door anyway. *"Gyaaaaaaaaaaaa!"* screamed the student in extreme pain, and with that realized enlightenment. Can you see that sect?

We always confuse the form with the substance. The time was ripe, that was the key. The time was ripe for Tokusan. The time was ripe for the Buddha. The time was ripe for Ananda and Mahakashyapa. What does it mean when we say, "The time was ripe"? A turning word can be almost anything, and it doesn't make sense to anyone else. Rinzai shouts and the monk becomes enlightened. Nansen became enlightened (and deafened) by Baso's shout. "The time is ripe" is like critical mass—all it takes is one more speck and the whole thing collapses. It is like in the poem: "Mountains have crumbled level with the plain."

RINZAI SHOUTS AND THE MONK BECOMES ENLIGHTENED.

"The Buddha's robe spontaneously entered Ananda's head." We chant every morning: "Vast is the robe of liberation"—that is the kesa. "A formless field of benefaction / I wear the Tathagatha's teaching / Saving all sentient beings." How is the kesa the Tathagatha's teaching? How is it the teaching of suchness? The teaching of "thusness"? How is it a "vast robe of liberation"? When one receives the

118

kesa, one receives a visible symbol of what is given in the precepts, the definition of the life of a Buddha, to practice with. What is given is the lineage from Shakyamuni Buddha through the successive generations down to your teacher's name and one's name in a line, which then circles right back to Shakyamuni. The lineage is a gigantic circle with all of the ancestors, beginning with Shakyamuni Buddha, to Mahakashyapa, to Ananda, and to all the successive generations in India, China, Japan, and America, to you, and then back to Shakyamuni. What you do is identify yourself with that life, that lineage, that bloodline. You say, "That life is my life." See? Mount Gudhakutra is very much present on this mountain. That is the meaning of "the robe entered the head of Ananda."

When Kashyapa instructed, "Take down the banner at the front gate," Ananda, because he realized the communion of teacher and disciple, was greatly enlightened. After enlightenment, he took down even Kashyapa, and the mountains and rivers all crumbled away. The Buddha's robe naturally came into Ananda's forehead. Master Keizan warns us, however, "Do not go by this incident to remain in the state of standing like a mile-high wall in the lump of red flesh. Do not linger in purity. You should go on to realize that there is a valley spirit. The Buddhas have appeared in the world one after another, the ancestral teachers pointed it out generation after generation. It was only this matter." That "mile-high wall" is a phrase used a great deal in Zen. It means being identified with and merged with the whole universe, no separation. It is what enlightenment is—to have forgotten the self and be enlightened by the ten thousand things. "Do not remain in that state," is what this kindly old great teacher is telling us. Don't remain in "purity," he says to make it even clearer. In Theravada Buddhism, that is the last step. The enlightenment experience is the ultimate, the peak of the mountain, the great "mile-high wall where the air is pure, the view is boundless." There are no edges, everything is

"DO NOT LINGER IN PURITY."

merged into one, no separation. You are completely identified with everything. In Zen, however, that is a dead end.
How will we create that archive of sanity on top of a mountain peak, stuck in oneness? What will we do about the
starving millions, nuclear holocaust, the pollution of the
environment? What will we do about the twenty-first century if we are sitting alone on some mountain peak contemplating our navels while the world goes by? That is not
our practice.

So what do you do? Do not be stuck in purity. Come
down off the mountain. How do you come down off the
mountain? How do you proceed from the top of a hun-
dred-foot pole? There you are in all your glory, having
realized the oneness of the ten thousand things, having
forgotten the self—now what do you do? Recall the phrase
of Dogen Zenji: "To study the Buddha Way is to study the
self." That is where it starts. "To study the self is to forget
the self." That is where it takes you. "To forget the self is to
be enlightened by the ten thousand things." That means to
be a mile-high wall with no separation. "To be enlightened
by the ten thousand things is to cast off body and mind, or
to free one's body and mind and those of others." It

"NO TRACE
OF ENLIGHT-
ENMENT
REMAINS."

doesn't end there. "No trace of enlightenment remains,
and this traceless enlightenment continues endlessly."
That is what our practice is. That is what is depicted in the
tenth of the Oxherding Pictures, the coming down off the
mountain. Keizan says, "You should go on to realize that
there is a valley spirit." The mountain spirit, the absolute;
the valley spirit, the relative. Until that which has been
realized has been manifested in the world, in our daily life,
formal Zen training is not over. It is just beginning when it
reaches that realization, then it needs to be manifested. We
call it "holy buddhahood": "ragged of clothes, covered
with the dust of the world, I go to the marketplace."

"The Buddhas appeared in the world one after another.
The enlightened ancestral teachers pointed it out generation after generation. It was only this matter." It was not

the words or the ideas that described it, not the books that were written about it, not the bodhi tree, the smile, or the flower. What was it? What is it? Nothing but the self. That is what it means to "really be intimate with yourself." To be intimate with yourself is to see eyebrow to eyebrow with Ananda and Kashyapa, with the Buddha and all the successive ancestors.

> The wisteria has withered
> Trees have fallen down
> Mountains have crumbled level with the plain.
> Flooding cascades have overflowed their bank
> Fire flashes forth from the flint boulders.

This poem from Master Keizan's collection *Transmission of the Light* poetically describes the moment of truth that was Ananda's. This is the ripeness that was Ananda's state of mind. Everything had fallen away; nothing remained.

"Ananda!"

"Yes, Master!"

The bow had been drawn to its full length, pointing directly at the heart of Ananda. Then, the turning word: "Take down the flagpole. *Flooding cascades have overflowed their bank / Fire flashes forth from the flint boulders.* The whole comes alive, and the wonder of reality shines at this absolute moment, here and now, transcending time and space. This is the mystery of the truth of the meeting on Mount Gudhakutra, which is ever-present here and now. What more can be said? Already the words that attempt to describe reality mar it, make it something other than what it is. It still all remains to be done. It is time to double our efforts, to go further than we ever have before, to sit harder and longer than is possible. That is our bloodline. That is the dragon entering the water.

THE WONDER OF REALITY SHINES AT THIS ABSOLUTE MOMENT.

Let's do it. Let's do it together, and as one. Let's manifest the wisdom and the compassion that is the life of the Buddha. That is the life of Ananda, Mahakashyapa, the life of countless realized men and women who have preceded us and who have passed on this dharma so that we can have the opportunity to practice it in our own lives. There is only one way to repay their kindness, and that is to awaken, to not squander our lives. To keep it alive. To keep it alive in our own lives, and make it possible for other generations to follow us. That is what we're doing on this mountain. It is not just for us personally, but for all sentient beings. When you make yourself free, you free all sentient beings. If you want to save all sentient beings, you have to begin by saving yourself.

13

PAINTING SPRING

ADDRESSING THE ASSEMBLY, Master Dogen said:

My late master, Old Buddha [Tendo Nyojo], said, "The original face has no birth and no death; Spring is in the plum blossoms and enters into a painting." When you paint Spring, do not paint willows, plums, peaches, or apricots, but just paint Spring. To paint willows, plums, peaches, or apricots is to paint willows, plum, peaches, or apricots — it is not yet painting Spring. It is not that Spring cannot be painted, but aside from my late master, Old Buddha, there is no one in India or China who has painted Spring. He alone was the sharp, pointed brush who painted Spring. This Spring is Spring in the painting because it enters into a painting. He does not use any other power, but lets plum blossoms activate Spring. He lets Spring enter into a painting and into a tree—this is his skillful means. Because my late master, Old Buddha, clarified the Treasury of the True Dharma Eye, he correctly transmitted it to the Buddhas and ancestors who assembled in the ten directions of past, future, and present. In this way, he thoroughly mastered the eyeball and opened up the plum blossoms.

"JUST PAINT SPRING."

This was written on the sixth day, eleventh month, first year of Kongen, 1243, at Yoshimi Monastery, Yoshita County, Echizen Province. Deep snow, three feet, all over the earth.

Master Dogen is one of the spiritual giants of history and one of the greatest religious teachers of Japan. He was an incredible poet, mystic, and philosopher, compiling many of his major works in his thirties. This translation of "Plum Blossoms" is one of the ninety-three sections of *Shobogenzo (Treasury of the True Dharma Eye)*, his master work.

When you paint Spring, do not paint willows, plums, peaches, or apricots, but just paint Spring. What is Dogen talking about when he says "just paint Spring"? What is Spring? He says that "Spring is in the plum branch covered with snow." In that withered-looking single branch sticking out from under the snow at thirty below zero there is Spring. Why can't we see it? Why can't it be seen? "Even though the attainment of realization is immediately manifest, its intimate nature is not necessarily realized. Some may realize it and some may not." Just paint Spring. Master Dogen writes in another fascicle, *Genjokoan (The Way of Everyday Life)*, that "seeing forms with the whole body and mind, hearing sounds with the whole body and mind, one understands them intimately." By definition, "intimately" means that there is no separation. To be intimate means to be the thing itself. Jizo asked Hogen, "Where have you come from?" "I pilgrimage aimlessly," replied Hogen. "What is the matter of your pilgrimage?" asked Jizo. "I don't know," replied Hogen. "Not knowing is most intimate," remarked Jizo. At that, Hogen experienced great enlightenment. In intimacy there is no internal dialogue letting you know that you are sitting well or sitting not too well, constantly evaluating, comparing, analyzing, judging. The witness disappears—there is no body, no mind, no self, no other, no subject, no object. Not even the object of your attention exists.

"NOT KNOWING IS MOST INTIMATE."

When you are the thing itself, it pervades the whole universe. When the thing itself pervades the whole universe, the reference system that we use to evaluate, analyze, judge, understand, and know is gone. How can you possibly know? A student says, "I was in deep samadhi." I ask, "What was it like?" She says, "Well, it was all black and then I felt this and then I felt that." In deep samadhi there is no way to evaluate; there is no sense of time or space. There is "no eye, ear, nose, tongue, body, mind, no color, sound, taste, touch, or phenomenon, no world of sight or consciousness." What are you going to evaluate with? That is the intimacy that Master Dogen is speaking of. That's the intimacy of "when you walk, just walk; when you cry, just cry; when you laugh, just laugh."

"WHEN YOU LAUGH, JUST LAUGH."

One of the koans of the Kamakura period (eleventh to thirteenth century) is similar on the surface to what is going on here. Artists and samurai warriors by the thousands flocked to the monasteries to learn Zen during the Kamakura period—the samurai because they were very concerned about being free from the question of life and death and had heard that these Zen monks had resolved it, and the artists because they had found that there was a particular kind of aesthetic in Zen that affected the way of perceiving painting, architecture, sculpture, and so forth. What we do here at Doshinji is very much a part of that Kamakura spirit, with the important distinction that we don't deal with what became in Japan a kind of watered-down version of Zen, diluted in order to make it palatable to artists. We don't dilute it at all. It is the whole thing—you get it or you don't get it. All the Zen literature and koans at that time, however, were written in classical Chinese, which very few Japanese could speak or read, and also required a profound understanding of Chinese poetry. Kamakura masters redid the koans to make them more Japanese as well as more understandable. One of these koans is called "Painting the Nature." It deals with Ichu, the seventh master of Jifukuji, a famous painter and Zen master. One day Nambutzu, a great warrior, came to see him and asked whether he could paint the fragrance described in a famous line of poetry, "After walking through the flowers, the horse's hoof is fragrant." Ichu drew a horse's hoof with a butterfly fluttering around it.

Then Nambutzu quoted the line, "Spring breeze over the river bank," and asked for a picture of the breeze. Ichu drew a branch of a waving willow. Nambutzu cited the famous Zen phrase, "A finger directly pointing to the human mind; see the nature to be Buddha," and asked for a picture of the mind. Ichu picked up the brush and flicked a spot of ink onto Nambutzu's face. The warrior was surprised and annoyed; Ichu rapidly sketched the angry face. Nambutzu asked for a picture of "the nature." Ichu broke the brush. Nambutzu didn't understand, and Ichu remarked, "If you haven't got that seeing eye, you can't see it." Nambutzu said, "Take another brush and paint the picture of the nature." Ichu replied, "Show me your nature and I'll paint it." Nambutzu had no words. There are test questions for this koan, including: How do you show the nature? Come, see your nature and bring proof of it! Say something on behalf of Nambutzu!

In this koan the questions and the way the master responded are at a very different level of understanding than what Dogen refers to when he speaks of his teacher, Tendo Nyojo: *It is not that Spring cannot be painted, but aside from our late master, Old Buddha, there is no one in India or China who has painted Spring. He alone was the sharp, pointed brush who painted Spring.* Painter, brush, canvas, image, subject—they are not many. The painter *is* the brush, the image *is* the painter, the subject *is* the object, the canvas *is* the paint. Those things only separate themselves when we separate them by the way we use our mind. Whether you are speaking of a painting, Mu, a tree, a Buddha, or a plum branch—how you see it, how you relate to it, has to do with how you live your life, with the question of life and death itself. *To paint willows, plums, peaches, or apricots is to paint willows, plums, peaches, or apricots—it is not yet painting Spring.* How do you paint Spring? *This Spring is Spring in the painting because it enters into a painting. He does not use any other power, but lets plum blossoms activate Spring. He lets Spring enter into a painting and into a tree—this is his skillful*

HOW YOU
SEE IT HAS
TO DO WITH
HOW YOU
LIVE YOUR
LIFE.

128

means. How do you manifest the sharp, pointed brush that paints Spring?

"To forget the self is to be enlightened by the ten thousand dharmas. To be enlightened by the ten thousand dharmas is to cast off body and mind, of self and other." The ten thousand dharmas is the whole phenomenal world. To be enlightened by the whole phenomenal world is to cast off body and mind of self and other. To be enlightened by the painting of Spring is to enter into Spring itself. Spring enlightens the painter, the painter enlightens Spring. Self is forgotten, Spring is forgotten. He lets the plum blossoms activate Spring; no other power is used. "Because my late master, Old Buddha, clarified the Treasury of the True Dharma Eye he correctly transmitted it to Buddhas and ancestors who assembled in the ten directions of past, future, and present. In this way, he thoroughly mastered the eyeball and opened up the plum blossom." The eyeball here is the Dharma Eye, the Buddha's eye. But how is it that his old master Tendo Nyojo thoroughly and correctly transmitted this "True Dharma Eye" to Buddhas and ancestors—the ones who preceded him, the ones who were in his presence, and the ones who followed him? He transmitted into the past, the present, and the future. Kasho Buddha, one of the legendary past seven Buddhas, died long before the Buddha was born. How is it that he transmitted to him? How is it that the act of realization penetrates both forward and backward? Every act of karma does that. We think of karma as affecting only the future, but it also effects the past and the present. If you want to understand the past, look at the present. If you want to know the future, look at the present. This very moment is past, present, and future. Mount Gudhakutra is here on this mountain. The Treasury of the True Dharma Eye of this very moment walks forward and backward in time.

He correctly transmitted it to the Buddhas and ancestors who assembled in the ten directions of past, future, and present. In this

SELF IS FOR-
GOTTEN,
SPRING IS
FORGOTTEN.

129

way, he thoroughly mastered the eyeball and opened the plum blossoms. What is the opening of the plum blossoms? It is being enlightened by the ten thousand dharmas, by the whole phenomenal universe. To be enlightened by the whole phenomenal universe is to "forget the self—to forget the self is to cast off body and mind of self and other. No trace of enlightenment remains and this traceless enlightenment continues endlessly."

This was written on the sixth day, eleventh month, first year of Konjen, 1243, at Yoshimi Monastery, Yoshita County, Echizen Province. Deep snow, three feet, all over the earth. "All over the earth" is right here now! The snowflake falls no place but here. No place but here is all over the earth—all over the universe. "Fields and mountains all taken by the snow / Nothing remains." "If doubt arises and you think that plum blossoms are not Gautama's eyeballs, you should consider whether anything other than plum blossoms should be seen as eyeballs. If you seek the eyeballs elsewhere, you will not recognize them even though you are facing them because the meaning is not consummated. This day is not this day of an individual, but it is this day of the great house. Right now you should realize the plum blossoms as eyeballs. Stop seeking any further." What does he mean, to realize the plum blossoms as eyeballs? There is a second translation of this passage: "If we're deluded and think that the plum blossom is not the enlightened eye . . ." Notice that what one translation expresses as "eyeball" another calls "the enlightened eye." The translation continues, "It is not the enlightened eye of Shakyamuni. We should ask ourselves if there is any other vision besides this. You should know that if you seek enlightenment outside of plum blossoms you will not get it even if it is right in your hands. Even if it is in front of your face, you will not see it. Today is not our day, but the day of the Buddha Way. Right now we must open up the enlightened eye of the plum blossoms and stop chasing after other things." The plum blossom—what is the plum blossom? What is the

"TODAY IS NOT OUR DAY, BUT THE DAY OF THE BUDDHA WAY."

130

opening of the plum blossom? What is Gautama's eyeball, the eye of the Buddha? How will you "just" paint Spring? People often say that the Soto school of Zen doesn't do koans, that it is the Rinzai school that uses koans. This is the master work of Dogen, founder of the Soto school in Japan, and just one of ninety-three chapters of the *Shobogenzo*. What we are dealing with is only three paragraphs of that chapter. In those three paragraphs are the following koans: What does it mean to just paint Spring? What is the sharp, pointed brush that paints Spring? How does Spring enter a painting? How does it enter the tree? How does he transmit to Buddhas of past, present, and future? What is it to master the eyeball and open the plum blossom? What is "deep snow three feet all over the earth"? What is the original face that has no birth or death? How does Spring in a plum blossom enter into a painting? These are all koans, and needless to say, explanations won't reach them. In face-to-face teaching, the thing itself needs to be presented. Live words, not dead words—turning words that reveal "body and mind have fallen away" . . . fallen away, fallen away, body and mind.

"Fallen away, body and mind" is not a zombie or corpse walking around, eyes rolled back, tongue pressed up against the upper palate, spaced out. It is alive, working, functioning, living, laughing, crying, dancing Zen, this very life Zen—the only kind of Zen there is. Zen is not an activity that takes place in the world; Zen is the activity of the world itself. To paint Spring, to paint the eyeball of the Buddha, is to manifest the Treasury of the True Dharma Eye. To transmit to the Buddhas of past, present, and future in the life each one of us is to realize. Tendo Nyojo, the Old Buddha, said:

> Bright and bright, clear and clear
> Do not seek only within the shadow of plum blossoms.
> Rain is created and clouds are formed
>   throughout past and present

Past and present, solitary and silent
Where does it end?

Clouds and rain are liberated from plum blossoms; past, present, and future *are* plum blossoms. Spring is activated from the power of plum blossoms. Where do you find yourself?

PART THREE
Valley Spirit

14

"NEITHER DIFFICULT NOR EASY"

Record of Layman P'ang: Case 3

POINTER

WHEN ONE IS ENLIGHTENED and enjoys perfect freedom of mind in ordinary life, one is like a tiger that commands its mountain retreat. If one is not enlightened and is battered about by worldly circumstances, one is like a monkey in a cage. If you want to know the Buddha nature, observe the times and the seasons, causes and conditions. Putting this aside, I ask you, how would you identify one who has mastered the Way?

MAIN CASE

Layman P'ang was sitting in his thatched cottage one day. "Difficult, difficult, difficult," he suddenly exclaimed, "like trying to scatter ten measures of sesame seed all over a tree." "Easy, easy, easy," returned Mrs. P'ang, "just like touching your feet to the ground when you get out of bed." "Neither difficult nor easy," said their daughter Ling Chao, "on the hundred grass tips, the Patriarchs' meaning."

VERSE

Difficult, difficult, difficult
Easy, easy, easy
Neither difficult nor easy
I say all three—wrong, wrong, wrong.
It is not difficult, it is not easy
It is not neither difficult nor easy
It is . . . you fill in the last line.

We are studying various koans and cases that are concerned with the so-called white-robed practitioners—lay students. The P'ang family is actually kind of remarkable; as you can see from this koan, even casual conversation around their dinner table was Dharma Combat. P'ang received dharma transmission from Master Matsu, and all of the family was reputed to be highly enlightened. There is a story that takes place when P'ang was on the road selling the bamboo baskets his daughter made as a way for the family to support themselves. They would only take out a day's worth at a time, selling just enough baskets to buy meals for that day. As P'ang was coming down off a bridge, he stumbled suddenly and fell roughly to the ground. When his daughter, Ling Chao, saw him fall, she ran quickly to him and threw herself to the ground. "What are you doing?" cried the Layman. "I saw Papa fall to the ground, so I'm helping," replied Ling Chao. "Luckily, no one was looking," remarked the Layman.

I was drawn to this particular koan as the subject for today's talk because of things that students have had to say in the interview room during this sesshin. One person comes in and says, "Oh, it's a great sesshin!" The next student comes in and says, "Oh, it's an awful sesshin!" Then someone else says it's neither good nor bad—on and on and on. Difficult, difficult, difficult . . . easy, easy, easy. Neither difficult nor easy. Absolute, absolute, absolute . . . relative, relative, relative. Neither absolute nor relative. Form, emptiness . . . stick, not a stick—all of the dualities.

How can they be resolved? What are they? The pointer says: *When one is enlightened and enjoys perfect freedom of mind in ordinary life, one is like a tiger that commands its mountain retreat.* What is "perfect freedom of mind in ordinary life"? Many people think of ordinary life as being something different from what happens here at the monastery; we need to realize that it is not different—that the activities of our ordinary life are not distinct from sacred activities. Freedom of mind means being able to function in all kinds of circumstances with no hindrance. In a sense, the monastery is just a training ground to enable us to manifest the dharma in everything we do, wherever we may be. A unique aspect of the training at our monastery is that it is not considered complete until we have "come down off the mountain" and have manifested "in the marketplace" what we have realized.

WHAT IS "PERFECT FREEDOM OF MIND IN ORDINARY LIFE"?

The practice of the clergy, particularly in our lineage, has also served as an example of this merging of the ordinary and the "holy." Most of the teachers have been married, have had families. It is difficult to teach about the practice of ordinary life unless you are living ordinary life. What we do here is very ordinary. We do what everybody else does in the world; the only difference is that we do it all within a practice matrix. The practice is an extraordinary process of "seeing" what it is that we are doing. It is this "seeing" that liberates us in our ordinary daily activities, that indeed reveals the sacredness of ordinary activity. *When one is enlightened and enjoys perfect freedom of mind in ordinary life, one is like a tiger that commands its mountain retreat. If one is not enlightened and is battered about by worldly circumstances, one is like a monkey in a cage.* What are the worldly circumstances that batter us about? What is the cage that encloses us? It can definitely seem like it is "out there." We can almost always make a good case that the fault lies elsewhere, that the responsibility lies somewhere outside ourselves. We can even develop a logic to back that conclusion up, and get agreement from most people that

137

this is the way things are. The fact remains, however, that the deeper we go into our practice, the more we realize

ALL OF THE BARRIERS WE CREATE ARE NOTHING BUT OUR- SELVES.

that there is no outside and that all the barriers we create are nothing but ourselves. When we say to "be the barrier," this is just another way of saying to return things to their original place, to bring things back into accordance with reality. The ten thousand things—barriers, enlighten- ment, Mu, all the koans, all the Buddhas and Patriarchs included—are not outside the self. It is when we place them "out there" and thus separate ourselves, that we cre- ate problems. This is true not only in terms of difficulties, but also in terms of wonderful things.

One of the worst defilements of the precepts, what is called "defiling the Three Treasures," is to simply give rise to the thought that there is a difference between Buddhas and ordinary beings. Even to harbor the thought that there is something special about a Buddha violates the pre- cepts. Being really clear on this point becomes particularly important when one has realized oneself after struggling for years, then struggled many years more to clarify that realization.

I am not, however, talking about what is known as Buji Zen. "Why do I have to do anything? I'm already there," says the novice standing in shit up to his nostrils and won- dering how he got there, why life is so awful and he's so miserable that he wishes he was dead. The fact is that standing in shit up to your nostrils *is* the dharma, but there is a big difference in mouthing that, believing it, having it up in your head—and having fully realized it. When you fully realize it, it is no longer a hindrance. Life is no longer a hindrance; death is no longer a hindrance. The reason it is no longer a hindrance is that it is not outside the self. The reason that it is not outside the self is that there is no self; the self is empty. It is not hard to repeat the words "The self is empty." None of these things is particularly difficult to understand or verbalize; scholars have written volume upon volume on Zen, and all it takes is a good memory to parrot the phrases and explanations. In our school, however, that has never worked. There are many renowned Buddhist scholars, people who write much of what we read on Buddhism, who have never practiced in their lives. There is a major difference between understanding the words and realizing the dharma—all the difference in the world.

If you want to know the Buddha nature, observe the times and the seasons, the causes and conditions. Let's look carefully at this phrase. One of the most useful guidelines I have experienced in this training, particularly with regard to the precepts but not limited to them, is the set of "Four Positions" taught by Yasutani Roshi: time, place, position, and degree. I am not certain that he originated them, but he is the one from whom my teacher received them. Every action that we take, every decision that we make, should be considered in terms of these four positions. The time that the action is taking place—the time of year, the time of day, and so on—is an important consideration. What is appropriate at one time is not appropriate at another time. What will cause conflict at one time works freely and easily at another time. The second consideration is the place that an action happens, its environment. Again, what is appropriate in one place at a particular time may not be appropriate at the same time in another place. When the place changes, the action changes, the effect of the action changes, and the karma changes.

The third consideration is of one's position. When an action takes place, it does so with respect to a particular position. It is always happening in the relativistic world. What one does as a teacher is very different from what one does as a lover, which is very different from what one does as a parent, which is different from what one does as a child. It is the same person, but the position changes with respect to the circumstances. There is no way to make a viable set of rules for what you should do, because what you should do is always determined by time, place, posi-

WHAT YOU SHOULD DO IS ALWAYS DETERMINED BY TIME, PLACE, POSITION, AND DEGREE.

tion, and degree—by a consideration of how much action is necessary. Sometimes it is necessary to shout, sometimes just to say a gentle word. Sometimes a strong action is necessary, sometimes a very easy action. Just the right amount. You know what to do. Look at the circumstances and at those four positions, and you know precisely what to do. The consequences can be vastly different according to how you act. It requires being conscious, being aware of times and seasons, of causes and conditions.

There is also another meaning to the phrase "being aware of the times and seasons, causes and conditions." What it points to is beautiful—"the evening clouds, endless / The distant hills, blue heaped upon blue, peak upon peak." These very mountains themselves are the body of the Buddha. The sound of the mountain stream is the voice of the Buddha, the voice of enlightenment expounding the dharma. A monk once asked a teacher, "I'm new here, how can I enter the Way?" The teacher said, "Listen, do you hear that stream?" The monk said, "Yes, I do." The teacher said, "Enter there."

Putting all of that aside, how would you identify the one who has mastered the way of the absolute? How do you understand these three people—Layman P'ang, Laywoman P'ang, and their daughter, Ling Chao? Sitting at home in his thatched cottage one day, Mr. P'ang suddenly exclaims, "Difficult, difficult, difficult . . . like trying to scatter ten measures of sesame seeds all over a tree." "Easy, easy, easy," returns Mrs. P'ang, "just like touching your feet on the ground when you get out of bed." "Neither difficult nor easy," says Ling Chao, "on a hundred grass tips, the Patriarch's meaning." What is the truth? Is it easy, is it difficult?

WHAT IS THE TRUTH? IS IT EASY, IS IT DIFFI-CULT?

In the *Sutra of the Third Patriarch*, it says that the Great Way is "neither easy nor difficult, it only avoids picking and choosing. But those with limited views are fearful and irresolute; the faster they hurry, the slower they go. Clinging (attachments) cannot be limited, even to be attached to the idea of enlightenment is to go astray. Just let things be in their own way, and there will be neither coming nor going." But we say, "How can I do that? I'm responsible; I'm in charge. I can't let things go their own way. If they did, the whole place would be in a mess." Difficult, difficult, difficult. When two people experience exactly the same phenomenon, exactly the same action, one can be totally overjoyed by it and another totally depressed by it, yet the same thing is going on. It is like a sesshin. For one person it is incredibly painful, yet for the person sitting on the next zafu, it couldn't be more wonderful. During the next sesshin, the situation may be reversed, with the happy student feeling awful and the miserable one happy and content. Why? Where does the movement come from? Two weeks ago, you wanted to die, everything was intolerable, nothing was working out. Here it is two weeks later, and everything is wonderful. When you really examine the circumstances nothing has changed. All the things that were awful last week are still there, but somehow they are not so awful anymore. All the reasons you wanted to die last week are still there but you don't think you should die now; you want to live forever. How is it that the change happens? How do we create that kind of karma? That's what is meant by "being battered about by circumstances." Those circumstances are nothing but ourselves. It is not the event "out there" that's doing it—there is no outside. The event is ourself. How we perceive it and our relationship to it determine our experience of it.

CIRCUMSTANCES ARE NOTHING BUT OURSELVES.

What is it that the P'ang family is talking about in this koan? What is it that is "easy," "difficult," "neither difficult nor easy"? They could be talking about any duality. Layman P'ang could be mumbling, "Empty, empty, empty . . . no place to stand." And Mrs. P'ang could be saying, "Full, full, full . . . everything is the Buddha's teaching." And Ling Chao could say, "Neither empty nor full!" It is the same dilemma—self and other, good and bad, pain and no pain, life and death, up and down. The truth of the matter

141

is that it can't be found in either of the extremes. Why? Because neither of the extremes exists. That is what Ling Chao was saying with "neither easy nor difficult." But I say that it is *not* difficult, *not* easy, and *not* neither difficult nor easy. Then what is it?

Difficult, difficult, difficult / Easy, easy, easy / Neither difficult nor easy / . . . All three are wrong. Where does the truth lie? How do you finish the verse? If it is not difficult, not easy, not neither difficult nor easy, then what is it? Ling Chao said, "Neither difficult nor easy . . . on a hundred grass tips, the Patriarchs' meaning." The "Patriarchs' meaning" refers to a recurrent question in Zen koans: "What is the meaning of Bodhidharma's coming from the West?" There are hundreds of answers from hundreds of different masters. When the monk asked Joshu, he said, "Cypress tree in the garden." Baso said he was tired, Chizo said he had a headache, Hyakujo said he did not understand. Baso said, "Chizo's head is white and Hyakujo's head is black." Kyogen said that it is like a man up a tree holding on by his teeth. Someone underneath asks, "What's the meaning of Bodhidharma's coming from the West?" If he opens his mouth to answer, he falls to his death. If he doesn't open his mouth, he fails the dharma. How do you answer? The answer *is* the meaning of Bodhidharma coming from the West. To see that koan is to answer that question. How do you answer when a person in a dream asks, "What is the meaning of Bodhidharma's coming from the West?"? I know a person who can write the meaning of Bodhidharma's coming from the West using the sky as the paper, Mount Sumeru as the brush, and the ocean as an inkwell. If you can do it, I open my bowing mat to you and bow. Each of these koans deals with the same question, and in each one of them, the answer is different. What does she point to with "on the hundred grass tips, the Patriarchs' meaning"?

In another encounter Ling Chao was questioned by her father, "A man of old said, 'Bright, bright, the hundred

"WHAT IS THE MEANING OF BODHIDHARMA'S COMING FROM THE WEST?"

142

grass tips; bright, bright, the Patriarchs' meaning . . . how do you understand this?" "What a thing for you to say in your ripe old age," admonished Ling Chao. "Well, what would you say?" asked the Layman. "Bright, bright, the hundred grass tips, bright, bright, the Patriarchs' meaning," replied Ling Chao. The Layman laughed. What was communicated there? How do you understand that?

The meaning of Bodhidharma's coming from the West is like asking the question "What is Truth?" or "What is Reality?" Indeed, what is Mu? What is life? It is very easy to think that these koans are some kind of esoteric abstractions, particularly when you are hearing them for the first time. It is hard to see their relevancy immediately. They have nothing to do with two thousand years ago, or Layman P'ang—they have to do with 1987, Mount Tremper, New York City, Boston. They have to do with the twentieth century, and with the twenty-first century. They are pointers for a way of using your mind and living your life. It is not enough to understand them, to imitate them, or to believe them—we have to realize them, to make them our own experience, and to manifest what is realized in the way our lives are lived. Only then do we give life to the Buddha; only then can we impart strength to others. Until the heart of the matter is thoroughly and clearly realized it is just a sham, a charade. The deeper you go into yourself, the deeper you go into the whole universe. When you realize the self, you realize the universe. When you realize the universe, you realize Mu. When you realize Mu, you realize yourself. Mu, self, other, universe, past, present, future—they all have the same home; they all return to the same place. When the world is destroyed, *it* remains indestructable. What is *it*? It is not difficult, not easy, not neither difficult nor easy—then what is it? It is important to find out for yourself. When you do, you make yourself free. When you make yourself free, you make all sentient beings free. That is how to realize the Four Bodhisattva Vows we chant each day. "Sentient beings are numberless, I vow to

KOANS ARE POINTERS FOR LIVING YOUR LIFE.

save them." Save yourself and you save all sentient beings. Free yourself and you free all sentient beings. Why? Because there is no separation between self and others. When you realize no separation, the ten thousand things return to the self, where they have always been whether you realize it or not. Stop looking elsewhere—the answers and the questions come from the same place.

15

Medicine and Sickness Cure Each Other

THE GREAT MASTER UNMON said: "Medicine and sickness cure each other. The whole earth is medicine. Where do you find the self?" There are all kinds of medicines and all kinds of sicknesses. In fact, just about every medicine I am aware of is also a poison if used in the wrong way, at the wrong time, for the wrong person, or in the wrong strength or dosage. It is interesting that the things which determine whether something is medicine or sickness have to do with a reference system of time, place, position, and degree. These considerations are a useful set of guidelines for making decisions about what to do because they provide a way to reflect on appropriateness of action. A certain dosage may be deadly, while at another dosage the same material is a useful medicine. Many immunization inoculations, for example, are the disease itself in dilute form. The very disease that would kill you is also the disease that can create immunity. The same principle is at work in the treatment of those allergies treated by slowly administering increasing dosages of the allergen over a period of time. Healing is a function not only of medicine and science, but also of spiritual practice. Buddha was a teacher and a healer, as were Jesus and Moses. Most of the great spiritual teachers of human history were also healers.

MOST OF THE GREAT SPIRITUAL TEACHERS WERE ALSO HEALERS.

147

It is a different kind of healing in a sense, and yet it is the same as physical healing.

The moral and ethical teaching of the Buddhist precepts are an example of this. They are sometimes referred to as a "golden chain." Gold dust is very valuable, yet if you get it in your eyes it can be painful and blinding. The golden chain of the precepts is healing and nourishing, yet it also can be a sickness or bondage if we attach to it. This is true not only of the ethical teachings, but even of enlightenment itself if we attach to it. To give rise to the thought that there is a difference between enlightened beings and ordinary beings is a grave spiritual sickness. Meditation can also be a disease. There is a sickness of meditation and a meditation of sickness. There is a sickness that heals meditation, and a meditation that heals sickness. Finally, there is the meditation and sickness that heal each other. The same can be said of all the dualities. Where do you find yourself?

Unmon said, "Medicine and sickness cure each other. The whole earth is medicine. Where do you find the self?" How will you find your way out of this? With the whole body and mind twenty-four hours a day concentrate on this towering mile-high wall you call self. What is it? Those who don't know what it really comes down to misunderstand it as "medicine and sickness merging with each other." For forty-nine years in more than three hundred assemblies, Shakyamuni Buddha adapted his teaching according to the sickness—all of this was giving medicine in accord with the disease, like exchanging sweet honey for bitter roots. The whole earth is medicine. Where will you sink your teeth into this one? If you can sink your teeth in, I guarantee you that you'll have a place to turn around and show some life. Then you'll see Unmon in person. If you look around and hesitate, you're a million miles from seeing it. Look! Unmon is right under your feet. Medicine and sickness cure each other. This is just common language, straight talk. If you think it is some kind of esoteric

THE WHOLE EARTH IS MEDICINE.

dialogue, you're sadly mistaken. What Unmon is saying is as relevant to our lives as each breath we draw into our lungs. It's not something to be understood or believed, though; it needs to be *seen*, to be realized by each one of us.

Unmon is saying that right now this whole great earth is a profuse array of myriad forms, up to and including ourselves, and at once, it is all medicine. At such a time, what do you call yourself? If you only call it medicine, you are ten thousand miles away from it. You still won't have seen Unmon even in a dream. Ultimately, how is it? Manjushri once said to his disciple Sudhana, "If there is something that isn't medicine, bring it to me." Sudhana searched all over but couldn't find anything that wasn't medicine. He went back and told Manjushri, "There is nothing that is not medicine." Manjushri said, "Then bring me something that is medicine." Sudhana picked a blade of grass and handed it to Manjushri, who held it up, showing it to the assembly, saying, "This medicine can kill people and it can also bring people to life." Do you see Manjushri's double-edged sword? One edge of the blade kills, and other gives life. This killing is the death of the ego, of the idea that we are separate and distinct from everything else. When the ego is dead, a new kind of life begins. This is why it is said that when you see the true nature of yourself, there is no way that you can live your life in the old way. It may take a long time to actualize it, but once you see it, it is like an itch that needs to be attended to. Once we see what is real, it's very difficult to hide from reality. Before we see it, we can plead ignorance and kind of bungle along, deluding ourselves about our existence. We can blame it on our parents or the president or any number of people, places, and things in order to avoid our responsibility. We can always be a victim, like the unfortunate soul caught in the "winds of circumstances." When you realize yourself, all of that self-deception is ended because you find out who is really responsible. It is *you*. You are the responsible party. There is no one else, nothing else. There is nothing

"THIS MEDICINE CAN KILL PEOPLE AND IT CAN ALSO BRING PEOPLE TO LIFE."

to be found outside yourself. At first, it is an awesome realization to be responsible, to have no one to blame anymore. It sounds silly if you try to say, "He made me angry," or "He made me do it," or "It's her fault." It sounds ridiculous, once you have realized yourself, to make the statement "I'm just a victim of circumstances." You realize that you are the circumstances, that you create what you experience, that what you do and what happens to you are identical. You realize that cause and effect are immediate and instantaneous; cause doesn't precede effect, nor does effect follow cause. If you want to know the past, look at this moment. If you want to know the future, look at this moment. This moment is the future and the past. Where will you find this moment? Who is this moment? What is this moment?

THIS MO-
MENT IS THE
FUTURE AND
THE PAST.

It is very easy to get caught up in emptiness. It would be very easy to spend the rest of your life in a trance called meditation, shutting out the world, sitting up on some mountaintop contemplating your navel and letting the world go by, but this is not our practice. When you are caught in nonexistence, the teacher points to existence. When you are caught up in existence, the teacher points to nonexistence. All of the extremes miss it.

> Front, back
> Front, back
>   falling autumn leaves.

What are the autumn leaves? Are they "front" or are they "back"? Are they neither "front" nor "back"? The autumn leaves are the medicine. How do you understand "autumn leaves"? Where do you find yourself? In the activity of this life itself are both the sickness and the cure. The way we practice here, our set of habit patterns, is no different from the way we do everything else in our life. If you want to heal everything else, this is a good place to start the healing. Pay attention to how you practice, how you sit. Our karma, the cause and effect of our lives, is all the "baggage" that we carry. It begins with the self. Where do you find yourself? The body is sickness. Where is its medicine to be found? Anger is the sickness. What is the cure? The karma of pain, of life and death, is the illness. How will it be healed? Mind is the disease. Where will you find the medicine?

We constantly polarize things, pull them apart, attach a label and file them. Then we define our reality accordingly. This is why for some people money is evil, poverty is good, enlightenment is wonderful, delusion is awful, Buddhas are great, ignorance is awful. This is a very deluded view. It is lopsided, and that is sickness. To even raise the thought that there is a difference between Buddhas and ordinary creatures violates the precepts and profanes the dharma. It creates the illusion that there is something to attain, something to teach and something to learn—something "outside." We need to get rid of all that we're holding on to. If part of that holding on is enlightenment, we need to get rid of that too. When we've gotten rid of everything and nothing is left, then we have to get rid of that too. "Nothing is left" is just another idea. As nice as it is, it's a sickness when you hold on to it.

We talk at times about the makyo that sometimes arises during long periods of zazen. If you sit for a long time without moving your body, all kinds of odd sensations occur. The most common one is the "off" sensation that can develop when you're not getting any physical messages of where your body "is." Normally, the friction of clothing on skin creates a sense of the outline of your body. In sitting motionless day after day, all day long, you don't get those messages. You're sitting there, and you know you have a body, but you can't feel it anymore. At first, you move just to verify that your body is still there, which is reassuring. Perhaps you feel yourself rising off the pillow, or suddenly you perceive the room as bathed in soft light, or you see the Buddha appearing before you. Makyo can be a sickness if we hold on to it. Many times people think makyo is

"NOTHING IS LEFT" IS JUST AN-OTHER IDEA.

enlightenment, particularly if the Buddha appears bathed in light. They get all excited and think they have had an enlightenment experience and usually run into interview to test it. Usually what a teacher will do is listen to the whole description and then say something like, "Well, you're probably not sitting straight. Why don't you sit a little straighter?" or "Breathe a little deeper, it'll go away, just don't hold on to it," and ring the bell ending the interview. It is the holding on to it that is the makyo. It's simply a hallucination, no different from any other kind of hallucination. When you go without eating for a long period of time, you begin to produce histamines in the body, which can cause you to hallucinate. Or, if you go without sleep for a long period of time, you will begin to hallucinate. Unfortunately, some people have actually formed whole teachings on the basis of makyo. They stop eating for two weeks and have all kinds of visions and sensations, and the next thing you know, there are a hundred followers trying to get the same visions and sensations.

Be that as it may, it is not our practice. We don't encourage people to fast during zazen. We don't encourage them to torture their bodies. Asceticism is not what our practice is about. Determination, yes; but asceticism, no. Definitely not. Shakyamuni Buddha's practice was a reaction to asceticism. You can see how this wonderful practice can very easily turn into a disease. We should keep our bodies healthy, get enough sleep, get enough food, and sit strong like a great granite mountain. The medicine changes in accordance with time, place, position, and degree.

ASCETICISM IS NOT WHAT OUR PRACTICE IS ABOUT.

Americans like to refer to one of the old Zen stories about how a Master took a wooden Buddha image, chopped it up, and made a fire, warming himself by its flames. Seeing this, a monk asked, "What are you doing, setting fire to the Buddha?" The Master replied, "Where is Buddha?" The opposite goes on in America. In America we want to burn the Buddha images to begin with. You see, that monk was stuck in the image, stuck on the form. In

America, we are antiform, so the pointing goes in another direction. If you're attached to neither existence nor non-existence, you manifest a sixteen-foot golden Buddha in a pile of shit and rubbish, appearing and disappearing.

"Medicine and sickness cure each other. All the world is medicine. Where do you find the self?" To realize the ultimate principle and not study is "to open the eyes in darkness." To study but not realize the ultimate principle is "to have the eyes closed in the bright light of day." To both realize and study the ultimate principle is "eyes open in broad daylight." We always tend toward the extremes, thinking that it has to be one end or the other. The Buddha Way is the middle way. It keeps pointing in the other direction, wherever we're sticking, whatever the extreme is. Our practice is the practice of flexibility, of having no position, fixing nowhere, holding on to nothing. In the process of arriving at that point, we stick everywhere. We are constantly sticking. We come into our practice stuck in all sorts of things, and slowly we begin to peel those away and replace them with new things. Sometimes I imagine it as trying to pull flypaper off people. Every time you reach to help them, you get stuck with it yourself. The teacher and the student are both stuck in the flypaper, getting it off the student. We let go of the Mercedes, and we attach to a robe; we let go of the robe, and we attach to attainment; we let go of attainment, and we attach to something else—on and on, back and forth. The thing that makes it so foolish is that everything is in a constant state of becoming. Nothing is fixed. The moment you attach to it, it changes. There you are holding on to something that no longer exists, regardless of whether it is a person, a place, a thing, or an idea. It is easy not to attach to material things. It is even easy not to attach to people. We have a very difficult time, however, in letting go of our ideas, concepts, and opinions. We will die for them. What a shame. Indeed, what a shame.

THE MO-
MENT YOU
ATTACH TO
IT, IT
CHANGES.

153

The great master Setcho prepared a verse for this koan of Unmon:

> The whole earth is medicine:
> Why have the ancients and moderns been so
>   mistaken?
> I don't make a carriage behind closed doors—
> The road is naturally quiet and empty.
> Wrong! Wrong!
> Though they be as high as the sky,
>   your nostrils have still been pierced.

"The whole earth is medicine. Why have the ancients and moderns been so mistaken?" From ancient times until now, those who have understood by calling it "medicine" have instantly gone wrong. There was an ancient master who, when he was about to die, said, "Coming, there is nothing to look to; going, there is nothing to pursue." Happening to hear a cry of a squirrel, he said, "It's just this thing! Not anything else. Keep it well—I'm going to go," and then he died. What Setcho has to say about this is, "This fellow was sloppy in life and fat-headed in death. 'Just this thing, not anything else'—what thing is this? Is there anything to impart, or not?" Indeed, what is "just this thing"? Is there anything to transmit? It is said that when Shakyamuni Buddha held up the flower on Mount Gudhakutra, out of the entire assembly of thousands of monks, nuns, and laypersons, only Mahakashyapa smiled. What if *everyone* had smiled? Whom would he have transmitted the dharma to? What if *no one* had smiled? What would have happened to the dharma? If you say there is no transmission, then Shakyamuni Buddha is making a fool out of all of us. If you say there is a transmission, then why only Mahakashyapa? Remember the ugly duckling/swan story? It is like approaching an entire flock of swans and saying to one of them, "You are a swan." The rest of them are excluded. How do you understand that?

"IS THERE ANYTHING TO IMPART, OR NOT?"

It's easy to say all of this. If you read enough over a period of years, you'll have all the dialogues down well;

you could also do that by going to college and studying Buddhism 101 or taking Ch'an Buddhism 603. But understanding it isn't going to liberate you. Study alone does not provide the power to cut the roots of delusion. You can talk all you want, understand all you want, but all it does is increase the bondage. You can even *believe* all you want, and then we'll have a generation of "Zen believers" for the first time in history. None of it means a thing until it has been realized. You have to *realize* it; you have to *manifest* "all the world is medicine" with your own life. Then you have the strength to make yourself free and impart strength to others; otherwise, you are like a ghost living in the body of a human, never fully realizing the human potential. To be born a human is an incredible gift. What a waste to spend this life jousting with windmills and chasing after shadows. It only takes a moment to realize yourself, to make yourself free, to heal yourself. Until you heal yourself, you can't heal others.

"Sickness and medicine heal each other. The nose ring still pierces your nostrils, though they may be high as the sky." It is because they are as high as the sky that they are going to get pierced by enlightenment. Like the bull with a nose ring, you get led around by your "holy" nose. "Vast emptiness, nothing holy." How do you understand that? Does that mean burning Buddhist statues or bowing to them? Or neither burning nor bowing? Ignoring? What does it mean? Nothing holy, vast emptiness. The precepts are medicine; the precepts are poison. *Samsara,* the world of confusion and anger, is medicine; samsara is poison, sickness. "The whole earth is medicine. Where do you find yourself?" What is the self? Who are you? If you're not clear on this point, you should find out. It is the most important thing we can do. Saving all sentient beings begins with yourself. Do it, not just with your head, with your ideas—but with your life. In broad daylight, with your eyes wide open, see it! Do you understand?

"SICKNESS AND MEDICINE HEAL EACH OTHER."

16

PICKING AND CHOOSING, COMING AND GOING

THE GREAT WAY is not difficult;
It only avoids picking and choosing.
When love and hate are both absent,
Everything becomes clear and undisguised.
Make the smallest distinction, however,
And heaven and earth are set infinitely apart.
If you wish to see the truth,
Then hold no opinions for or against anything.
To set up what you like against what you dislike
Is a disease of the mind.
When the deep meaning of things is not understood,
The mind's essential peace is disturbed to no avail.
The Way is perfect like vast space,
Where nothing is lacking and nothing is in excess.
Indeed, it is due to our choosing to accept or reject
That we do not see the true nature of things.
Live neither in the entanglements of outer things
Nor in inner feelings of emptiness.
Be serene in the oneness of things
And such erroneous views will disappear by
    themselves.
To deny the reality of things
Is to miss their reality;
To assert the emptiness of things

Is to miss their reality.
The more you talk and think about it,
The farther astray you wander from the truth.
Stop talking and thinking
And there is nothing that you will not be able to know.

This passage is from *The Faith Mind Sutra: Verses on the Unfailing Source of Life* of Master Sozan, the third Zen Patriarch in China, the dharma "grandson" of Bodhidharma. It deals with faith in mind, faith in how the mind really functions. Later in the sutra, Master Sozan says:

One thing, all things,
　　move among and intermingle without distinction.
To live in this realization,
　　is to be without anxiety about nonperfection;
To live in this faith is the road to nonduality,
　　because the nondual is one with a trusting mind.

EVERY-
THING
THROUGH-
OUT SPACE
AND TIME IS
INTER-
CONNECTED.

One thing, all things, move among and intermingle without distinction points to the unfailing source of life that he refers to in the subtitle. It is what we call the Diamond Net of Indra. Everything throughout space and time is interconnected, and at each connection—at each point—is a diamond that reflects every other diamond throughout the four dimensions, so that in this vast net, each diamond contains every other diamond. This is one thing, all things, moving among and intermingling without distinction. The diamond net is "the unfailing source of life." Indeed, it is life itself, your life itself. We separate ourselves from this unfailing source of life with our mind, our thoughts, our ideas. The only way you can separate yourself is mentally, because "one thing, all things, move among and intermingle" is the way it is, whether we realize it or not. Regardless of whether we live our lives according to this or not, the fact remains that it is the way things are. With our minds we separate ourselves and immediately create all the dualities of life. On one side we create pain, greed, anger—fun-

158

damental ignorance. We also create the other side—joy, compassion, wisdom, and enlightenment.

When love and hate are both absent, everything becomes clear and undisguised. When duality is absent, everything becomes clear. But we shouldn't cling to this "clarity" either. The other side of clarity is confusion; both are diseases of the mind. All of the dualities are mutually arising; they are all co-dependent. You can't have one without the other: good and bad, heads and tails, heaven and earth. That is why it is said, *Make the smallest distinction, . . . and heaven and earth are set infinitely apart.* They are not set apart until we separate them in our minds (and by "we" I do not mean only Westerners—the same thing holds true of people in China, Japan, India, and every place else). Civilization itself is founded on the dualistic use of the mind. The Buddha went beyond dualism, beyond the distinction between this and that, to show that there is no self, that what we call the "self" is a creation of our own consciousness which separates us from everything else.

Picking and choosing, coming and going, love and hate, inside and outside, having and not having, accepting and rejecting, asserting and denying, form and emptiness, right and wrong—they all begin with making the smallest distinction. They all begin with the idea of a separate self, a boundary between the self and the rest of reality, an inside and an outside. Coming and going is such a difficult and painful process. Our lives are filled with the pains of coming and going: coming into a relationship, a marriage, a new job, a new place; leaving a relationship, a marriage, a job, the place where you live. We do not seem to understand how to execute these life functions without creating pain, anger, or confusion. We are tearing ourselves away from some imaginary thing that we stick to—that by its very nature cannot be stuck to or torn away from. Coming is always right here and right now. Going is always right here and right now. It is because there is no coming and no going that we can speak of coming and going.

IT IS BECAUSE THERE IS NO COMING AND NO GOING THAT WE CAN SPEAK OF COMING AND GOING.

159

Because of that illusion of separateness, we find it hard to come and go. We find it difficult to come together, difficult to part. I know many people who have had wonderful relationships, but because of the time, the circumstances, or various changes in their lives, they have had to go their separate ways. To be able to do that, somehow the creation of anger is usually necessary. There is that need to feel justified, to have a reason to separate. Since love is what brings us together—that is our rationale—then hate must be what will drive us apart. So we create anger. It is unnecessary, and so poisonous. Coming and going is a functioning of life, like waves rising and falling. We can learn to come and go without coming and going. We can learn to avoid picking and choosing. So how can we avoid picking and choosing, coming and going? Just to open our mouths to speak is picking and choosing. Just to say "avoid picking and choosing" is picking and choosing. What kind of practice avoids picking and choosing? Avoids coming and going?

This suffering, this picking and choosing, this painful coming and going, is related to ignorance. Master Sozan says, *It is due to our choosing to accept or reject that we do not see the true nature of things.* Later in the sutra, he tells us, "The changes that appear to occur in the empty world we call real only because of our ignorance." Ignorance means not knowing what is real. It is very easy to get totally lost in the confusion between the apparent and real. In a way, our lives are based on that confusion, on our fundamental assumption of a separate self, an assumption that is simply false. The consequence of this basic premise, and all the delusive thoughts that arise from it, is suffering in its multitude of forms. The practice that avoids picking and choosing, coming and going, is the practice that avoids dualism, that brings us back to the ground of our being.

IGNORANCE MEANS NOT KNOWING WHAT IS REAL.

The great Master Joshu very often used this *Faith Mind Sutra* of Master Sozan to teach his monks. One day a monk asked him: "It is said that the Great Way is not difficult; it only avoids picking and choosing. Now, what is not picking and choosing?" Joshu said, "I alone am holy throughout heaven and earth." The monk responded, "That is still picking and choosing." And Joshu said: "Asshole! Where's the picking and choosing?" The monk was speechless.

Joshu answered him with the words of the Buddha: "I alone am the Honored One between heaven and earth." He is saying there is nothing outside of me; I am the Diamond Net of Indra. In a sense, that is picking and choosing, but only when you are coming from a position other than the position Joshu was standing in. The monk was standing outside of that, and from his point of view he was justified in saying, "That is still picking and choosing." Position is everything. Everything changes, even when the circumstances remain identical, when you shift your position. Try it sometime with someone who is an adversary. Shift your position. Be that person, and the adversary disappears. Shift positions with whatever barrier you are facing in zazen, in your life. Be the barrier, and it is no longer there. It is only there because we pull back, separate ourselves from it. The more we pull back, the bigger and more overwhelming it gets, and the angrier or the more frightened we become. If we really look at the anger that makes us crazy, or the fear that stops us cold, we see that it develops step by step from our thought process. And the starting point of that thought process is separation. Is the cause of the fear something that might be lurking in a dark alley? The possibility of falling down and breaking your neck? Losing your job? No, it is yourself. When you really acknowledge that it is nothing but yourself, when you realize this fact, you can not live your life in the old way. You've suddenly taken responsibility for it. Before, the problem was outside—your bad luck, what others did to you, the circumstances you could do nothing about.

When you realize that the cause is you, you empower yourself. You suddenly become ten thousand feet high— you fill the universe. There is no picking and choosing,

EVERY-
THING
CHANGES
WHEN YOU
SHIFT YOUR
POSITION.

"I ALONE
AM THE
HONORED
ONE BE-
TWEEN
HEAVEN AND
EARTH!"

coming or going—no place to go, no place to come from. Joshu was trying to show the monk that "ten-thousand-foot-high Buddha." But the monk was standing in a different position. So Joshu yelled, "Asshole!" Actually the Chinese word is usually translated as "country bumpkin" or "stupid oaf," but this sounds too tame for our ears. It was meant to shock, to stun the monk into experiencing the reality of what the Buddha said: "I alone am the Honored One between heaven and earth!" Nothing is outside of you.

Joshu was coming from the position of the absolute, which would become a kind of blindness if he stuck there. But when the monk said, "That is still picking and choosing," Joshu shouted, "Asshole! Where's the picking and choosing?," immediately shifting positions, slamming right into that monk from the relativistic standpoint. He was showing him: you and I are the same thing, but I am not you and you are not me. We should not stick anywhere—not in the relative, not in the absolute.

> To deny the reality of things
> is to miss their reality;
> To assert the emptiness of things
> is to miss their reality.

Sticking to clarity, to enlightenment, is the worst kind of delusion. In Zen there is going beyond clarity, "no trace of enlightenment remains and this traceless enlightenment continues endlessly." Going beyond clarity, not abiding in it, is very ordinary. There is no stink of Zen about it, no holiness to hold on to.

In that vast Diamond Net of Indra, each thing contains everything, and each thing is separate and distinct from everything else. Thinking, talking, and doing are the ways we create our lives, the ways we create our karma. We can see how our actions create cause, and we can see that every cause has consequences. The same is true for our thoughts. It is because of our interconnectedness, our intermingling and moving among this one thing, that it works in that way. Because of that, talking and thinking and doing can create karma. We can use it to poison or to nourish, depending upon how we manifest it. How do we manifest it so that it nourishes, so that it heals? By nontalking, nonthinking, nondoing. How do you do "nonthinking" and "nondoing"? How can you possibly avoid picking and choosing?

> The more you talk and think about it,
> The further astray you wander from the truth.
> Stop talking and thinking
> And there is nothing that you will not be able to know.

Stop knowing and not-knowing. Knowing is another kind of holding on, of separation; not knowing is blank consciousness, emptiness. How do we avoid these extremes of form and emptiness, enlightenment and delusion? By learning to be ourselves, but not self-consciously, not passively. "Be serene in the oneness of things" does not mean "Watch the world go by" or "Do not do anything." That is not what Sozan is talking about, and it is not what our practice is. Being yourself means giving yourself permission to be who and what you are. That is "faith mind," having faith in your true self, trusting yourself. Until that happens, you cannot really trust anything or anybody. When you have that trust, your defensiveness disappears. You don't need to be arrogant or to put yourself down, to hide, or to withdraw. These two extremes are the same thing, different ways of protecting that idea of a separate self. Being yourself, being intimate with yourself, is the beginning of intimacy with all things. Being yourself is "no separation."

BEING YOURSELF IS "NO SEPARATION."

> The Great Way is not difficult:
> Direct word, direct speech.
> In one, there are many phrases:
> In two, there is one.

Difficult, difficult,
Picking and choosing, coming and going.
Be still, watch,
See for yourself.

17

THE SACRED TEACHINGS OF WORK

Those who regard mundane life as an obstacle to dharma know only that there is no dharma in secular activities; they do not yet know that no secular activities exist in dharma.

—MASTER DOGEN

I WOULD LIKE TO TALK about work practice, how our ordinary daily tasks can become opportunities to practice. When students reach a certain point of maturity in zazen, their work, their life, everything they do develops an equivalent clarity and integrity. Work emerges as an active function of zazen and provides an opportunity to examine our habits, our way of doing things.

WORK IS AN ACTIVE FUNCTION OF ZAZEN.

The selflessness taught and practiced in a monastic environment tends to conflict with the self-indulgence generally encouraged in our society. In the zendo, we bow to each other; in the subway, we push each other. In the monastery, we serve; in the world, we take. The monastery can begin to take the form of a sanctuary—but it is more like a furnace within which, through our training, we can forge a life of strength, gracefulness, and self-confidence to meet the situations we each face every day. Our practice is not about isolating ourselves on some mountaintop, dwelling in tranquillity while rejecting the busy activity of the world, but manifesting the Buddhadharma in everything that we do, so that the secular is indeed the sacred. This is what we need to see in order to make the practice of work function as an aspect of our Zen training.

There are many ways to practice work. We can look at it as just "a job to be done," or as simply a way to pass the time, to prevent boredom or idleness. We can also look at it as a sacred activity, as a manifestation of the miracle of being alive. What we practice in the zendo is the "heart of the matter," the core that needs to express itself in everything that we do. Zazen is not just sitting cross-legged on a pillow; it is growing a garden, getting to work on time, getting the job done.

WORK IS A MANIFESTATION OF THE MIRACLE OF BEING ALIVE.

The foundation of work practice is mindfulness, a state of consciousness in which the body is relaxed, the senses are alert, and the mind is clear and focused on the task at hand. This attentiveness is direct experience. Mindfulness is not static; it moves with the events in our daily life. There are times when we need to totally put ourselves into the task at hand: this is "holding fast," single-pointedly concentrating. At other times, it is necessary to "let go," to release and move on. Our tendency is to stick, to move on to the next thing, still carrying all the debris of the last thing with us. Mindfulness develops the ability to flow, concentrate, and remain in the present.

Some people have the misconception that planning and scheduling are not what Zen Buddhists do. But planning is not goal-oriented—it exists right now; scheduling exists right now. Without a plan, our work tends to become very scattered, inefficient, and ineffective. We can get caught up in goals and forget that the goal and the process which brings us to that goal are the same reality—just as "good" and "bad" are the same reality, just as heads and tails are two sides of the same coin. Each step, each action that brings us closer to the goal, is the goal itself. One is not before and the other after; they both exist simultaneously. When we fully realize this, then our preoccupation with the goal disappears and we can be fully aware of the pres-

EACH STEP IS THE GOAL ITSELF.

ent moment. Then, each step is vivid, each step can be experienced totally.

One of the important parts of work practice is preparation, the placing of everything required for the job in a state of readiness. The work, tools, and materials are laid out. A number of years ago I began a process of ritualizing my preparations to photograph by taking very deliberate steps in laying out my camera, film, light meter, and other equipment, putting it all together, getting ready to go out and photograph. I found that the process was also putting my mind in a state of readiness, awareness.

The Zen arts are highly developed forms of work practice. In teaching a Zen art, theory is rarely dealt with. The art is taught and communicated by practice itself. For example, the teacher of *sumi-e* often does not speak a word in his first meeting with his students. The class sits and waits; the master enters, bows to the students, and then proceeds to his work space. There, he carefully lays out his equipment, the paper, the brushes, the ink tray, and the ink stick, and begins to examine the tools to select the ones he will use. Then he adds a bit of water to the tray and begins rubbing the ink stick in the tray very slowly, producing the ink. This process is itself a meditation; each breath corresponds to one stroke in mixing the ink. When the right consistency, thickness, and tone have been produced, he sets the stick aside, selects a brush, and carefully examines the blank paper. He sits in the presence of the empty space on the paper, feels the space, realizes the space fully. Then he wets his brush with just the right amount of ink and in a single breath executes a *zenga* painting, a whole landscape. The entire process may take half an hour to forty-five minutes of preparation and clean-up time, but the actual production of the painting takes place in a single breath. Those who have the opportunity to observe such masters at work can see their single-pointedness of mind and attention to detail. There quite clearly are characteristics common to all these masters regardless of whether we are

ZEN ART IS TAUGHT AND COMMUNICATED BY PRACTICE.

speaking of a painter, a master of the bamboo flute, or of the martial arts: a kind of spontaneity, professionalism, and free-flowing action is inevitably evident.

Work practice can also be a teacher if we regard it that way; the teaching is everywhere if we have eyes to see it. The rocks and water of the river expound the dharma daily, if we have ears to hear. The bringing of the palms together in gassho used so frequently in the monastery is a reminder that all of the dualities are part of the same reality. The left and the right hand come together as one thing: no separation. When I bow to the salt, I acknowledge that the salt and I are one thing. When I bow to you, I acknowledge that you and I are the same thing. When I bow to the Buddha, I acknowledge that it is the Buddha bowing to the Buddha. And so it is with work. After the work is laid out, the next step is doing it. The art of this step is to really "do what you are doing while you are doing it." In other words, to be fully present. To experience the breath in zazen, be it . . . be the koan . . . be zazen itself. To be the work is no different.

When the work is finished, there is a sense of completion, just as there is a sense of completion when you have finished a painting, a photograph, a performance. It is time to let go. Time to bow and acknowledge the teaching. It doesn't matter whether you are bowing to something animate or inanimate; in either case, you are bowing to yourself. There is nothing outside you, unless you put it outside yourself, and you can only do that by the way you use your mind. To really complete it, clean up, put the tools away, pick up the loose ends, "leave no trace." This means the dishes are washed and put away, the counters are wiped, the sink is clean, the floor is swept and mopped, the garbage is emptied. No trace remains that someone has eaten. Everything looks natural and ordinary. Of course, this also means not being excessive about it: "no trace" means no trace.

We also face problems in work practice that function as

CLEAN UP, PUT THE TOOLS AWAY, "LEAVE NO TRACE."

the koans of our everyday life. They can be handled in the same manner as the koans we work with in zazen. How do you deal with problems when they come up when you are sitting in the zendo? It is like when you are sitting, staying with your breath, and you hear a sound that reminds you of something that reminds you of the next thing, and the next thing, and suddenly you are a thousand miles away and the breath has been forgotten while you become immersed in whatever scenario you are developing. When you realize that you are not involved with the breath any longer, but are involved with a thought: you look at the thought, acknowledge it, let it go, and come back to the breath. You don't evaluate it, analyze it, love it, or hate it. If the thought pops up again, you go through the process again: look at it, acknowledge it, let it go, and return your attention to the breath. Each time you bring the attention back to where you want it, you reinforce your power of concentration. And if the thought continues to recur, you let it happen. Be it. If fear keeps coming up, be the fear. Allow it; give it free range. Be the thing itself; don't separate from it. Each time you separate from it, it gets bigger. The more you pull away from it, the more powerful it becomes. Then, after it has exhausted itself, completed its cycle, let it go and return to the breath.

BRING THE ATTENTION BACK TO WHERE YOU WANT IT.

The same process takes place with work practice. Each time you become distracted, you acknowledge what is happening, let the thoughts go, and return your attention to your work. Sometimes in work practice just like in zazen, we get "stuck." This is what interview is for. You can use interview as an opportunity to look at and work with the problem in a different way. It becomes a koan. And the koans that rise out of our own sitting or out of our work are oftentimes the most powerful koans of our life. A problem is just another name for an opportunity to really put yourself into your practice. It is easy to practice when everything is going smoothly, but to sit *hard* is to sit when sitting is difficult. It is also the place that generally is the most productive, because the things that are most difficult for us almost always have the most to teach us.

Another aspect to consider in work practice is silence. Silence doesn't mean not speaking when it is necessary, in answering the phone, in giving instructions, but just cutting down on the unnecessary chatter, the talk that is there just for the sake of talking. When it is necessary to speak in order to communicate, we should do so; when it is time to be silent, we should be able to do that, too. This means being not only outwardly silent, but also silencing the inner dialogue, our habit of constant talking to ourselves. Practicing silence and avoiding idle talk helps develop the clarity, receptiveness, and concentration necessary for good work practice.

SILENCE
THE INNER
DIALOGUE.

This way of working is not "spacy," preoccupied, or trancelike; it is very much alive, filled with life's force, awake, and alert. It is the mind of the Way itself. What is the mind of the Way? Indeed, what is the Tao? Joshu once asked Nansen, "What is the Tao?" Nansen answered, "Ordinary mind is the Tao." "Then should we direct ourselves toward it or not?" asked Joshu. "If you try to direct yourself toward it, you go away from it," answered Nansen. Joshu continued, "If we do not try, how can we know that it is the Tao?" Nansen replied, "The Tao does not belong to knowing or to not knowing. Knowing is illusion; not-knowing is blank consciousness. If you really attain to the Tao of no doubt, it is like the great void, so vast and boundless. How, then, can there be right and wrong in the Tao?" Ordinary mind: the mind that sleeps when it is tired and eats when it is hungry. This is the Buddha mind, the mind of work practice.

Layman P'ang said, "Isn't it wonderful? Isn't it marvelous? I chop wood and carry water." We should see that this life itself and all of its activity are the perfect manifestation of the Buddhadharma. This very life is the life of the Buddha, and the secular activities of this life are the dharma itself. But we should be aware, as Master Dogen says, that "to carry the self forward and realize the secular is delusion; that the secular advances and realizes the self is enlightenment." To "carry the self forward" means to separate yourself. That the "secular advances" means to be one with the object of your attention. The secular world itself becomes your life, and its inherent liberation is constantly manifested. If you still do not believe it, consider your breath for a moment. Bring it in from the atmosphere that surrounds you, taste it, fill your body with it, enjoy it. Now let it go, return it to the environment—isn't it a miracle, this life of ours?

ISN'T IT A MIRACLE, THIS LIFE OF OURS?

18

THE ART OF SEEING

This chapter is edited from tapes of a Zen arts retreat on "Mindful Photography." Students were seated in the workshop room facing a projection screen that presented an abstract photographic image.

BEGIN TO RELAX THE BODY by first closing your eyes and becoming aware of the muscles of the face, particularly those around the eyes. Become aware of any tension that may be there. Then deliberately and consciously let go of that tension. Now the muscles of the jaw. Relax any tension there so that the jaw hangs loosely and the tongue is resting against the roof of the mouth. Now the muscles in the back of the neck—feel them relaxing. The muscles of the back and shoulders, the muscles of the chest. Feel those muscles and be aware of any tension that may be there. Let go of it. Now become aware of your breathing. It is deep and easy, without effort. Imagine each inhalation bringing energy into the body and each exhalation as letting go of tension. Let go of any tension in your arms, your hands . . . and the muscles of the thighs, calves, and feet.

Imagine a small pond, and, with your eyes closed, try to see it—a small pond with a white swan floating on it. Very still. No movement. No wind. No sound. Try to feel the stillness with your whole body. Try to contact that still

NO MOVE-MENT. NO WIND. NO SOUND.

175

place within yourself that connects with the pond and the swan. Now become aware of your *hara*—the area two or three fingers below the navel. Give all your attention to that point, and begin drawing energy from all the parts of the body to that single point. From the top of your head, the tips of your toes, the tips of your fingers—all the energy of your body is coming to focus at that point just below your navel. Feel it building there—a feeling of lightness. Now begin to move that energy upward to the back of your eyes. Hold it there and feel it building. There is a light feeling of pressure there.

Begin by taking a flash look at the image on the screen—rapidly open and close your eyes. With your eyes closed now, work with the after-image. See the image that is left when you closed your eyes, and be aware of how you feel—not what you *think* about the image—just be aware of how you feel. Next open your eyes and engage the image fully. See the whole thing at once without thinking about it, without trying to identify, judge, analyze, understand. Simply see it, experience it. How does it feel?

BE AWARE OF HOW YOU FEEL—NOT WHAT YOU THINK ABOUT THE IMAGE.

Now we can begin to examine the image in detail. Let your eyes slowly scan the image, seeing everything. Leave nothing out. Be aware of what happens to your feelings as your eyes move to different parts of the image. Do they change? Do they stay the same? Try to postpone judgment. Just see and feel.

Now begin to enter the image. Imagine yourself moving into the image: walking into it, floating, jumping, diving into it—it does not matter how—moving about on its surface. How does that feel? How does the space around you feel? What does it feel like underfoot? Be aware of all the senses. Do you feel hot or cold? Do you feel roughness or smoothness? Is it wet or dry? Are there any odors? What part of the body is affected? See if you can go deeper into the image—become part of it. How does that feel? Go beyond the borders, beyond the frame. How does that feel? Moving back inside the frame, what do you feel? Now begin to move back out of the image, and be aware of your feelings as you do that. Are they the same? Do they change? See the image again as a whole, all at once, without looking at the details. Be aware of how that feels. Now take one last look, close your eyes, and be aware of the feelings that remain.

SEE THE IMAGE AS A WHOLE, ALL AT ONCE.

Now, as we finish, become aware of the point just below the navel again and draw the energy from behind the eyes back toward that point. Feel it building there. There is the same feeling of lightness—then deliberately and consciously let go of it. Let go of the image, let go of the feelings. Become aware of yourself, the room, the sounds inside and outside the room. Make small movements, and slowly open your eyes.

What we have done is the first part of a process called Creative Audience, a way of looking at an image that is intimate and experiential rather than critical and discriminatory. In the second part, we will be sharing our experience as audience with the creator of the image. When you have created an image—a photograph, a painting, a sculpture, or whatever—you have no way of knowing how anyone else experiences it. With the kind of creative feedback we will be giving, we begin to know the experience of both audience and creator. It will go both ways—sometimes you will be in one role, sometimes in the other. As an artist, you can broaden your way of seeing and clarify what it is that you are communicating to the audience—whether your images are nourishing or poisonous, how other people see things in relation to how you see them. And you can begin to see an image as someone else sees it.

An image you have created is a very intimate thing—it is part of its creator's guts—and to share that is a difficult process. As audience, your experience of an image is a very intimate thing, and to share that is a difficult process. For it to work, we must enter into this process in a spirit of openness. Each of us has to reach down past the barriers and distances within us and between us and give as much

WE MUST ENTER INTO THIS PROCESS IN A SPIRIT OF OPENNESS.

as we can of our experience of the image. And the job of the person receiving the information is to hear it—really hear it, to be receptive, to try not to screen it through preconceived ideas about the image—to really hear what is being communicated. So what we are interested in is your experience, not your ideas, not your concepts—just how you felt. Anyone want to start?

STUDENT: I felt breezes and coldness. I felt myself rolling around on its surfaces, and rolling in snow. But the other parts were like rolling in mud. It was comfortable, warmer—when I tried to go beyond the frame, I saw cliffs and rocks. It was cold and smelled fishy, like the ocean. Off one border there were dangerous cliffs, but on the other side it's more like deep water. Outside there's a feeling of darkness and being afraid. Going back inside was like going back to a warm comfortable place, I did not want to deal with whatever was outside.

SECOND STUDENT: I am afraid of the white areas, especially in the center where it sparkles. I felt secure near the top where there is texture, but the white seems too bright, like the Arctic. I just had a feeling about the white—I did not want to look at it, I guess—and when I got too close to the border, I felt resistance. There seemed to be something dangerous beyond that—a place where I should not go. Or did not want to go.

WITNESS EACH FEEL-ING AND THEN GO ON.

THIRD STUDENT: When I go into it, it suddenly changes into something effervescent and bubbling. I want to dive into that sparkling, cool spring. When I moved outside of the frame, I was drifting toward something like sunlight—warm and very peaceful.

One of the things that happens in working with images is that all kinds of feelings come up: good feelings and bad feelings; frightening feelings, angry feelings, and loving, open feelings. What we've got to learn to do, as we experience a feeling, is to make a notation, witness it. To witness means simply to be aware of it and then to go on, not to let this barrier we've created stop us from going any further. We have to let ourselves experience the fear or the dislike or the strangeness, not shut ourselves off from it. When you look at somebody's photograph and you do not like it right off, you do not want to see it anymore and you close it off. Our tendency in life is to do the things we like and avoid the things that we dislike, or do things we understand and not try things we do not understand. As a result, the process of discovery cannot happen—you cannot discover until you go past what you have already experienced. So when you run it through the computer in your head, if it is familiar, safe—if it is OK—you continue with it. If not, you close the door. But it is where we are not familiar, where we are frightened to go, where we hate going that has the most to tell us. In fact, the very process of hating or fearing or whatever—that is the information. So it is good to let ourselves experience the fright—note it and go right through it and let it happen. The way we usually block the experience is by thinking, creating mental images around it. These thoughts protect us from experiences that threaten our ego, our sense of separate self.

It is very helpful, in looking at an image, not to be able to identify what it is. If I had stepped back another two feet in making the slide photograph we used for this first session, the image would have included the four wheels that identify it as an overturned farm wagon. The underside had been exposed to rain and dampness and had several varieties of mold growing on it. If I had stepped back, you would have seen it as the moldy underside of a farm wagon, and a great many of the experiences you had would not have happened. Of course, it is possible to see what an image represents, to see the wheels—and still be able to experience the image directly and vividly. But we tend to let our concepts and ideas—the baggage of the self—close the door. The moment we can identify the image, we tend to stop seeing and we do not go any further.

WE TEND TO LET OUR CONCEPTS AND IDEAS CLOSE THE DOOR.

One of the things that we hope to develop in this process

is the ability to see things each time for the first time. The fact is that when we look at something, whether it is an object in nature, a photographic subject, or a created image, we are so programmed that we cannot really see what we are looking at. Even if it is something we have never seen before, our internal reference system goes to work fitting what we are seeing into a slot that we are familiar with. Once we have that familiar category, we plug into a whole reference system of the associations, feelings, information, and preconceived judgments that make up our life-long experience of it. We are conditioned to see in a certain way. What that conditioning does is protect and strengthen the idea of a separate self that we have been building, layer by layer, since infancy. We cannot see—see things as if for the first time, see things as they really are—until we let go of that idea of a separate self.

Letting go is something we have to learn little by little. The technique that we have been working with is a way to begin learning that. The process involves relaxing, letting go of the defenses we've locked into our muscles, quieting our minds, feeling our energy and moving it to the eyes, **RECEIVE THE IMAGE WITHOUT JUDGING.** receiving the image without judging, short-circuiting some of our conditioning, being completely with the image and aware of our feelings and sensations, then pulling the energy back, and consciously and deliberately letting go of the image.

Still, as you do this, there is a gap between you, as observer, and the image. The same is true of the feelings, resistances, and barriers that you experience. There is a gap between you as the observer and the experience that you are witnessing. We try to close that gap. You can do that most readily when the feelings are the most intense—you become the fear, the anger, the anguish, the joy. A very different thing happens once you become part of it, once you stop separating yourself from the thing you are experiencing.

STUDENT: I always found that instruction, "Try to become one with it, try to close the gap," very easy to understand, but . . .

DAIDO: Very difficult to do.

STUDENT: Yes.

DAIDO: The fact is, of course, that there really is no gap, and there never was. It is something we create with our minds, with our concept of separateness: of this and that, head and tails, up and down, me and it. If there is no me, then there is no gap anymore; there is nothing to create it. When you are seeing a tree and there is only a tree and no you—no self—you have let go of the self. There is no ground, sky, road, no noises, smells, no taste, touch, sound; there is only the tree. That tree becomes the universe—the universe is contained in a single tree. You are seeing things as they really are.

THERE REALLY IS NO GAP, AND THERE NEVER WAS.

19

Zen Mind, Well Mind

Quite a number of years ago in a psychology course, I came across what was called the "general adaptation syndrome," a description of the dramatic physiological changes that take place when a person is under stress. For instance, when you feel threatened, the body prepares itself for combat. The blood vessels are pulled back from the surface of the skin, so that if you are cut you do not bleed as much. Vision becomes very acute; strength is increased manyfold; reaction time is shortened; reflexes become very sharp—all because of adrenaline pouring into the bloodstream. This is a survival mechanism that has been with the human race since its beginnings. If you are face to face with a saber-tooth tiger, that reaction takes place, and either you fight for your life or you run. Either way you need that heightened power. Whether the stimulus is some clearcut physical danger or a more complex psychological situation that gets us tangled up in anxiety, anger, or frustration, the response to threat occurs to some degree, depending on the intensity of our feelings. If that power—that energy—is not used, there it is, racing around inside the body. You have no way to dissipate it.

WHEN YOU FEEL THREATENED, THE BODY PREPARES ITSELF FOR COMBAT.

That is the thing that causes problems, particularly when there is no resolution and the stress situation is prolonged. As it continues day after day, the body/mind begins to respond in its own individual way—with chronic tension, pain, or disturbances in breathing, heart function,

183

digestion, with chronic anxiety, depression, panic attacks, and so on. As it continues, the trouble will get more serious. It is becoming very clear that stress can play a major role in triggering cancer, heart disease, arthritis, and all sorts of other diseases, as well as mental breakdown.

So what do we do about it? We may withdraw, psychologically or physically—if we have the chance. We try to avoid stress by putting up a barrier of time or space, or some kind of mental barrier. Or we can take one of the hundreds of drugs prescribed for stress, or take illegal drugs, get stoned, or get drunk. We can make ourselves numb. Then there are therapeutic activities like running, aerobics, and massage, and the psychological therapies and the meditation therapies. It is true that these activities and therapies reduce stress. The big question is: do they ever really get to the root of it?

When you look at these therapies and the other ways of dealing with stress, you see that usually they have one thing in common. They are based on the assumption that the cause of stress and the effect of stress are two separate things. Either we are putting a barrier between ourselves and the apparent cause of the stress—drugging ourselves numb or running away in some other fashion—or we are trying to remove something or change something we believe to be the "cause" of the stress. But in actual fact, the cause of stress is not something "out there," and the cause and effect of stress are not two different things.

THE CAUSE AND EFFECT OF STRESS ARE NOT TWO DIFFERENT THINGS.

We need to go deeper to really look at stress, to appreciate how it functions and how we can work·with it as a fact of our lives. Life would be pretty dull without it. A lot of our vigor and alertness, and certainly the development of the species, has to do with dealing with stress, being stimulated by it. But when it reaches the point where it becomes unmanageable and starts debilitating us, then there is something wrong with the way we are dealing with it. And the basic thing that is wrong is the illusion of separateness, of a separate self.

184

When you ask someone, "What is the self?," the answer will usually be a list of parts or items—the self is this body/mind, my history, my memory, my thoughts. Our most basic assumption is that everything inside this bag of skin is me and everything outside of it is the rest of the universe. That does not deal with the question "What is the self?" What is selfness itself? Obviously, the self that you are now is not the self that you were when you were three months old. You are not the same psychologically, chemically, physically. You do not look, act, think, or feel the same. And you are not the self at eighty that you are at forty. So the self is, first of all, something that is in a constant state of transition, a constant state of becoming.

THE SELF IS IN A CONSTANT STATE OF BECOMING.

That much is easy to understand. We can see, if we look at all this evidence, that, like everything else in the universe, the self is not fixed, not permanent. But the other side of it, the fact that there *is* no self separate from everything else in the universe, is not something that we can arrive at logically through an intellectual process. The nature of this no-separate-self has to be experienced.

Zen training provides us with the means to do that. Through zazen, sitting meditation, we learn little by little to drop the intellectual processes, to let go of the thoughts, the fantasies, that block the direct, intuitive experience of who and what we really are. Our constant mental activity is what holds up the illusion of a separate self and makes us vulnerable to stress.

In zazen, the first thing we learn is to just be still. Most of us are constantly engaged in activity, either inner or outer. If we are not directly focused on some activity, there is a constant mental dialogue. We are talking to ourselves and scattering our energy. We are preoccupied with the past, which no longer exists—it has already happened. Or we are preoccupied with the future, which does not exist—it has not happened yet. We generate a tremendous amount of stress in this type of preoccupation. We worry about what has happened, about what will or will not happen in the future; we think about the various things that make us feel anxious, frustrated, angry, resentful, depressed, afraid. And while we are so preoccupied, we are missing the moment-to-moment awareness of our life. It slips by and we hardly notice its passing; we eat without tasting, look without seeing, listen without hearing, live without ever knowing—perceiving—what is real.

TAKE THE SCATTERED ENERGY AND FOCUS IT.

What we do in zazen is take the scattered energy and focus it. Zazen has to do with being in the moment, without evaluating, analyzing, judging—just simply and directly experiencing, moment to moment. In Zen, the way this is done is through the breath. The breath is directly related to mental activity. When your mind is agitated, your breath is agitated. When the mind is at rest, the breath is at rest. Zen practice begins with counting the breath—inhalation is one, exhalation is two, inhalation is three, and so on up to ten. When you get to ten, you go back to one and start again. The only agreement you make with yourself is that when your mind begins to wander—when you begin to chase thoughts—you look at that, acknowledge it, and let go of the thoughts. And start again at one. With practice—and it takes time to get from one to ten even once—the internal dialogue begins to quiet down. It is like learning anything else. If you want to learn to walk a tightrope, you string a wire across the room, you take one step and fall off, come back and take another step and fall off, and keep doing that patiently until at one point you suddenly take two steps and then three steps, and as the days go by you are finally able to walk across the tightrope. It is the same with calming the mind.

WHEN IT IS TIME FOR THE MIND TO SHUT UP, WE LEARN TO SHUT UP.

When it is time to think, we should think. When it is time for the mind to shut up, we should learn to shut up. Being able just to be still and shut up is a facility that just about every creature on the face of the earth has. Humans seem to have lost that ability—even in our sleep we are constantly agitated. Meditation is one opportunity to really come to rest.

In Zen training, when we get the surface mind quiet, a lot of the deeper stuff that we do not want to think about begins popping up. We have been talking to ourselves to avoid these painful thoughts and feelings, and when the mind becomes calm, we begin to be aware of them. But through zazen we develop a way of dealing with what we have been avoiding: we look at it—without analyzing or judging, we acknowledge it, let go of it, and go back to the breath.

Little by little, as concentration builds, and *joriki,* the power of concentration, develops. Your awareness becomes very acute. You begin to notice subtleties that you never experience when your mind is constantly going. When the mind gets quiet and empty of thoughts, you become very, very receptive. If the joriki becomes strong enough, samadhi happens: awareness of the body and of mental activity stops, and time loses its meaning. Samadhi is very refreshing, but it can also be a trap. It can also be a way of avoiding dealing with things or tuning them out. In Zen it is considered "dead-end samadhi" to stop in samadhi. To stop anywhere is a dead end.

SAMADHI IS VERY REFRESHING, BUT IT CAN ALSO BE A TRAP.

When samadhi develops, we usually introduce a koan. A koan is a nonlogical statement, question, or anecdote, most often an exchange between master and student from the Zen literature. A koan is a means for the student to confront the self, to bypass logical, conceptual thinking. It becomes the object of concentration. This first koan can take many forms. Classically in Zen it would be: What is your original face? The face you had before your parents were born? Show it to me. Or: You know the sound of two hands clapping—what is the sound of one hand clapping? Do not talk about it—show me!

These questions are no different from: What is truth? What is reality? What is life? What is God? Who am I? They are all the same question. They deal with the ultimate nature of reality, the ground of being.

Students sit in meditation with that question for many

187

months, sometimes many years, putting their whole body and mind into it. A koan is specifically designed to short-circuit the whole intellectual process; you cannot solve it intellectually, through linear sequential thought. That kind of thinking has to do with the left hemisphere of the brain. Seeing a koan has to do with the right hemisphere of the brain—it is direct, intuitive, immediate, does not operate sequentially, logically, rationally. So we sit with this koan, knowing that it can be resolved and having great trust and confidence in our ability to see it. In Zen one of the necessary elements is this Great Faith—knowing that you are going to see it, penetrate the question. Equal to this is what is called Great Doubt—the questioning that is always with you: What is it? Who am I? What is truth? What is reality? The third thing we have to bring to Zen practice is Great Determination. The barrier we face in dealing with a koan is the ego, that idea of self which is specifically programmed not to be forgotten. But in order to see the koan, we need to forget the self and become the koan—become our original face at this very moment. When we are locked inside a bag of skin, the koan is outside of us . We have to let go of that sense of separateness and be the koan.

WHEN WE ARE LOCKED INSIDE A BAG OF SKIN, THE KOAN IS OUTSIDE OF US.

Zen has to do with working through our conditioning, layer by layer, to reach the ground of being and experience it directly. That is what *kensho*—awakening—means: to see the nature of the self, to experience directly your own ground of being. Your way of relating to the universe and to the self is completely transformed when that is experienced. Once you have experienced it, you can never live your life in the old way.

But this realization is not the end of Zen training. Developing concentration and samadhi, sitting in meditation year after year, is like scaling a mountain. You struggle up the slopes, moving ahead a few feet, going on and on no matter how exhausted you are. Finally you reach the top, which is like the ground of being. But if you stay there, it becomes just as much of a delusion as anything else. You need to keep going—down the other side of the mountain, back into everyday life, into the marketplace. Until realization manifests itself—in the way we raise a child, grow a garden, drive a car, live our life—what the hell good is it? Zen has to do with everyday life.

ZEN HAS TO DO WITH EVERYDAY LIFE.

One of the things that is realized when you see the nature of the self is that what you do and what happens to you are the same thing. Realizing that you do not exist separately from everything else, you realize responsibility: you are responsible for everything you experience. You can no longer say, "He made me angry." How could he make you angry? Only you can make you angry. That understanding changes your way of relating to the world and your way of looking at stress. You see that stress is created in your mental processing of your experiences. It usually has to do with separation. Whenever a threat, barrier, or obstacle pops up, our immediate reaction is to pull back, to prepare mentally or physically to fight or run. If you become the barrier—become the fear, the pain, the anger—by experiencing it fully without judging or avoiding or running away, and then let it go, there is no barrier. Actually, there is no way to pull away from it; you cannot run away. There is nowhere to run to, nothing to run from: it is *you*.

None of the antidotes to stress—numbing ourselves, running away, the various therapies—will ever really get to the root of it. When we can acknowledge that we create our own stress and begin to look at how we create it, then we can begin to do something about it. Until then, we are just blaming, not taking responsibility. We say the trouble is my job, it is my boss, my wife, my husband, it is the kids, it is this, it is that . . . and we turn it into some kind of inner tension. We actually hold on to our stress. It is a way of holding on to our positions, our beliefs, our sense of being right—our self. In that tightness and rigidity, the body cannot deal with it and the mind cannot deal with it. We

189

suffer because we will not let go. In zazen we learn how to let go, to let go of thoughts as they come up. When we begin doing that, we find that we can begin to let go of tension, anger, fear, pain. We begin to build confidence, trust ourselves, and not be dependent on something outside. There is nothing out there—there is only you. And how you deal with what is happening in your head makes all the difference in the world in how you live your life.

When we can let go of the idea of a separate self that we carry around in our heads, we have begun to make ourselves really free. What keeps us from being free is the boundary we create around ourselves. Just as we create pain and confusion, we can change them. Just as we make our body and mind sick, so we can heal ourselves. And we begin at the beginning, with that simple process of quieting the mind, focusing it, letting go of our thoughts.

W E CAN HEAL OURSELVES.

20

"SAGES AND WARRIORS LIVING TOGETHER"

Blue Cliff Record: Case 35, *"Manjushri's Threes"*

MASTER ENGO'S POINTER

IN DISTINGUISHING dragon from snake, jewel from stone, black from white, irresolute from decisive, if one does not have the clear eye of the mind and the amulet under the armor, one invites instant failure. Just at this moment, if one's vision and hearing are clear, and color and sound are truly cognized, tell me, is he black or white, crooked or straight? The subtle difference—how can you discern it?

MAIN CASE

Manjushri asked Muchaku, "Where are you from?" Muchaku said, "From the south." Manjushri asked, "How is the Buddhadharma in the south?" Muchaku answered, "Fine. The monks follow the teaching faithfully." Manjushri asked, "How many?" Muchaku answered, "At some monasteries three hundred, at others five hundred. How about here?" Manjushri said, "Sages and warriors are living together. Dragons and snakes are intermingled." Muchaku asked, "How many?" Manjushri answered, "Front, three, three. Back, three, three."

MASTER SETCHO'S VERSE

The ten thousand hills,
Peak upon peak, deep blue.
Who can converse with Manjushri?
How I laugh at many or few.
How I admire Front, three, three;
   back, three, three.

IT IS THE REVEALING OF THE GOLDEN-FACED BUD-DHA IN OUR VERY LIVES.

Much of what we do in the practice of karate has to do with the point of this koan. Warriors and practitioners of the Buddha Way, living and practicing together: dragons and snakes intermingled. It is the revealing of the golden-faced Buddha in our very lives.

When he was a young man Muchaku traveled all over the country visiting various Zen teachers. The story that takes place in this koan is an incident occurring during his journey. He was a student of the great master Kyozan, and eventually succeeded him. As the story goes, Muchaku made a pilgrimage to Mount Gorba, a holy mountain in China long dedicated to Manjushri, the bodhisattva of wisdom. Manjushri has always been held in very high regard by Zen practitioners, all the way back to the time of the Buddha. Normally in a monastery, the image in the meditation hall is not that of the Buddha. The Buddha image is usually in the Buddha hall, where services are conducted. In the zendo, Manjushri is on the altar sitting astride a lion, and in his hand he holds the sword of wisdom, or prajna. It's a double-edged sword, a sword that can be used "to kill or to give life." When we say "kill," we mean kill the ego, the idea of a separate self. When we kill the ego we give birth to the Buddha nature and make ourselves free.

As the story goes, it was evening when Muchaku arrived on this mountain dedicated to Manjushri. He was in the middle of the wilderness with no buildings or houses or villages anywhere near. He found a temple at the foot of the mountain, and stayed there overnight. The master priest of the temple met him, and the conversation I just related took place. The next morning, when Muchaku was leaving, the master asked one of his students, a young temple boy, to see him off to the gate. When they were standing at the gate, Muchaku asked the boy who the master was and what the name of the temple was. Without saying anything, the boy pointed to the mountain. Muchaku turned to look at the mountain. When he looked back, the boy was gone, the temple was gone, and there was only wilderness. Muchaku realized then that the master priest had been Manjushri himself, who had appeared for the sake of his devotee.

This case has to do with absolute and relative and their mutual interpenetration. That's what this life is. The interpenetration of the practice of karate and Zen points to the same thing. In karate, the activity; in Zen, the stillness—not two separate things! In *The Heart Sutra* chanted each morning, we repeatedly say the phrase "Form is emptiness, emptiness is form. Form is exactly emptiness, emptiness exactly form." This, too, is pointing to the same principle. Body and mind are not two separate things, yet we separate them. We persist in thinking that they are two different things. The consequences are drastically different when you proceed on that assumption from what they are when you realize that there is no separation. Body and mind are one. It's the same with karate, "empty hand." What is "empty hand"? How do you wield the spear without using your hands? It's fundamental to the practice of karate to personally realize "empty hand." You can't realize empty hand until you realize empty mind. All of your thoughts, analyses, judgments, and evaluations get in the way—not only of this art but of any art. How can a musician truly be a musician if he's trying to figure out what he's supposed to do next? The piano plays by itself, the dance dances itself, the brush paints by itself. How to accomplish this is one of the key points in this koan.

When we start this practice, we first try to appreciate the

YOU CAN'T REALIZE EMPTY HAND UNTIL YOU REALIZE EMPTY MIND.

ground of being, the absolute basis of reality. We try to get past the illusion that this bag of skin is who we are, the idea that everything inside is me and everything outside is the rest of the world. It's not like that, and when you really see who you are, when you really experience directly the ground of your being, it is liberating, it makes you free. It makes you free of life and death. Surely, every warrior should be free of life and death, else how can you practice your art? You can't afford to cling to anything, least of all life and death. Once that absolute basis of existence is seen, and seen clearly, the next step is to see its relationship with the world of the relative. You and I are the same thing, yet I'm not you and you're not me. It's hard to make sense of that logically. How can it be that we're the same thing, but I'm not you and you're not me? As long as you approach it with logical, sequential thought, you're not going to see it. There is another aspect of your consciousness that you should be aware of. Each one of you has it. It is direct, immediate and intuitive. It's not sequential. It's like . . . [strikes lectern] . . . *that!* That aspect working freely keeps us from sticking anywhere.

EVERY WARRIOR SHOULD BE FREE OF LIFE AND DEATH.

The third part is to wipe all that away: absolute, relative, absolute and relative interpenetrating. That's what we mean when we say "coming down off the mountain and back into the marketplace." No trace of enlightenment remains, and this traceless enlightenment continues endlessly. Before we can deal with wiping out all the traces, before we can deal with absolute and relative interpenetrated, we first need to clearly see the basis of the whole thing. Most of us from birth are conditioned inadvertently by our parents, teachers, schools, culture, education, and peers. The main point of zazen is to get beyond that conditioning, beyond that robotlike existence where we respond to situations as if programmed. Deconditioning means reaching the ground of being, finding out who you are, learning to live your life out of your own direct experience. No one can tell you what it is. To tell you is just to give you another idea, and if you believe it, it's just another belief system. Realization has nothing to do with believing or understanding. It's got to do with realizing it with your own life. That's how you make yourself free. When you believe, you're attached to belief systems. When you understand, you're attached to words and ideas. Reality resides in neither of those; it's the direct experience of your very life that we're talking about. All phenomena are empty, yet all phenomena are functioning. How do you keep from falling into one or the other? If you call this a stick, you miss it. You're tied up in the words and ideas that describe it. If you say it's not a stick, you deny its existence. So what is it? Neither stick nor not a stick. Neither absolute nor relative. Neither heaven nor earth. What is it? Don't tell me about it. Show me! Make it your own experience, not an idea, not a belief. It's the same as your practice. You can be a great philosopher of karate, but that isn't worth a nickel when you're facing an opponent. You can't talk your way out of it, you have to be it! So how to do that? *Empty-handed.*

REALIZATION HAS NOTHING TO DO WITH BELIEVING OR UNDERSTANDING.

There's an interesting old Zen story about a great master who received the dharma transmission but didn't want to teach. He knew if he hid out in the mountains the monks would find him and start bugging him for the teaching, so he went to live with the bums who hung out under the bridges in Japan. He became a bum. But the emperor, one of the warlords, found out and wanted him as a national teacher, and instructed his soldiers to try to find him. Try as they might, they couldn't find him; all of the beggars looked basically the same. Then they contacted another Zen master for advice on how to find the man they were seeking. The master said, "Well, he really loves melons. Give your soldiers thousands of melons and have them go to each of the bridges and offer free melons to all the bums. Just as each one comes up to accept a melon, have a soldier say, 'Take the melon without using your hands,' and the true Zen master will reveal himself." So they did that. They went from bridge to bridge, and to each bum that came up a soldier would shout out, "Take the melon without using your hands!" Most of them didn't know what to do and would just look at the soldier like he was kind of weird. They'd give the bum the melon and he would leave and they'd go on to the next one. Finally, this master came up. The soldier said, "Take the melon without using your hands!" The master immediately responded, "Hand it to me without using your hands!" They nailed him. Of course, he didn't reveal what it means to take the melon without using one's hands; but he did test the soldier. How do you take the melon without using your hands? How do you take this stick away from me without using your hands? What is "empty hand"? What is "karate"? This is a key point. The power and force of your art come from really understanding this koan with your whole body and mind.

There once was a Zen nun whose husband had been a samurai killed in battle. She also was trained in the arts of the samurai. When her husband died, she shaved her head, went to a monastery, and became a really strong student. She actually succeeded her master and became the abbess of one of the temples during that period. One evening following *rohatsu* sesshin, which is the big winter sesshin with intensive meditation for eight days, she was returning to her monastery and was accosted by a man carrying a sword, who was intent on raping her. She reached into her sleeve and took a rolled-up sheaf of paper, and as he came close to her with his sword she let out a great shout and charged into him with the paper sword pointed right between his eyes. Her shout, her confidence and spiritual power, overwhelmed him completely. He fell down and scrambled up to his feet and began to run. And she never even touched him! She blinded him with fear, with her own power. That's why when you really accomplish this art, that power gives you confidence. When you have confidence, there is no arrogance, no anger, and no fear. The ego drops away. Strange as it may seem, this very

"TAKE THE MELON WITHOUT USING YOUR HANDS!"

WHEN YOU HAVE CONFIDENCE, THERE IS NO ARROGANCE.

198

powerful martial art in its ultimate form is very gentle. You don't need arrogance when you're in command of your life. "Be master of yourself," is what the Buddha says. Only you can do that. Only you have the power to make yourself free. In order to do it, you have to go very deep into yourself and find the foundation of your life, of your existence, of reality. Once you experience it for yourself directly, that experience is transformative. You can never live your life in the old way once having realized it. It is to not be stuck in the absolute, to not be stuck in the relative. It's to not be stuck in the profane or the holy. That is karate: *empty hand.*

A warrior came riding into the temple carrying a spear. The master of the temple said, "Are you a master of that spear?" "Yes, I am," the warrior replied. "How do you wield the spear without using your hands?" asked the master. The warrior had no answer. For months he stayed at the monastery and could be seen sitting in the meditation hall saying over and over to himself, "Karate, karate . . . be karate, be empty hand." Someone asked me if the warrior ever figured it out, and as I recall, he returned to battle and came back to the monastery badly wounded, with blood all over him. When he walked in, the master didn't take notice of the wounds or the blood, but immediately said to him, "What is karate?" The warrior still couldn't answer. He heard the call back to battle and returned. When he came back to the temple a third time he was mortally wounded, barely able to drag himself back through the temple doors. The master emphatically asked him, "What is karate?" Standing there, leaning on his sword, trembling, he let out a great shout and died standing on his feet. Now, that wouldn't satisfy the teacher in the interview room on the koan "What is karate?" but it does point to the determination that both karate and Zen practice require. In the words of the great master Bodhidharma, "Seven times knocked down, eight times get up." Without that spirit, there really isn't a chance of

"SEVEN TIMES KNOCKED DOWN, EIGHT TIMES GET UP."

199

accomplishing yourself. Determination and perseverance are the keys, along with great faith in yourself and great doubt—that driving question, "What is it?" "Who am I?" "What is empty hand?"

Look at Manjushri's words and realize *it*. Are Manjushri's and Muchaku's answers to the same question different or the same? Manjushri was testing Muchaku: "How many?" "Where are you from?" These are testing questions to discern the depth of the student's understanding. Muchaku asked the same questions of Manjushri. Manjushri said, "Warriors and sages are living together, dragons and snakes are intermingled." Muchaku asked, "How many?" When he was asked that, he said, "Five hundred in some monasteries, three hundred in other monasteries." Manjushri answered, "Front, three, three; back, three, three." What is he saying? What's the meaning of "Front, three, three; back, three, three"? What do a dragon and a snake have to do with it? What do "warriors and sages intermingled" have to do with it? What is karate? Don't tell me—*be it!* Be empty hand! It is not an idea. Whatever you think it is, it's not! It's not a word, it's not a thought. It's your very life itself! Until you manifest it there, you're like a phantom, a ghost. The way you make yourself free is by being it.

DON'T TELL
ME—BE IT!

Setcho's verse: *The ten thousand hills, peak upon peak, deep blue. Who can converse with Manjushri?* Right there is another key. How do you converse with Manjushri? Don't separate yourself! *How I laugh at many or few.* He's laughing because that's getting caught in the relative. *How I admire 'Front, three three; back, three three.'* Why isn't that caught in the relative or the absolute? How can you be yourself? How can you realize yourself? How can you make yourself free? How is it to manifest a life of peace and tranquillity in everything you do—driving your car, living your life, raising your children, growing your garden, practicing your art? How to do it? This is the most important question we can ever face. The most important thing you can ever do with your life is to realize yourself, to make yourself free.

> Beautiful this summer day.
> Endless the distant mountains,
> Blue heaped upon blue, peak upon peak.
> See? It's just like this!

Do you understand? If you don't, don't waste any more time. Find out. Tomorrow is too late. It never happens tomorrow. Find out right now. Make yourself free.

GLOSSARY

ANANDA   The cousin, attendant, and favored student of Shakyamuni Buddha. He is credited with an unusual memory and is said to have recited from memory all of the Buddha's discourses at the first Buddhist council convened after the death of the Buddha. Ananda was also responsible for persuading the Buddha to accept women into the monastic order.

ANUTTARA-SAMYAK-SAMBODHI   Supreme perfect enlightenment.

AVALOKITESHVARA   One of the principal Bodhisattvas in the Zen Buddhist tradition. Avalokiteshvara, said to hear the voices of all sentient beings, personifies boundless compassion and is usually represented in female form. In Japanese this Bodhisattva is known as Kannon or Kanzeon, in Chinese as Kuan Yin.

BLUE CLIFF RECORD   A collection of one hundred koans compiled, with appreciatory verses, by Master Hsueh-tou Ch'ung-hsien (Jap. Setcho Juken, 980–1052)) and with commentaries by Master Yuan-wu k'o-Ch'in (Jap. Engo Kokugon, 1063–1135). A key text in the Rinzai school, it was studied by Dogen Zenji, who carried a handwritten copy back to Japan from China.

BODHI MIND   Mind in which the aspiration for enlightenment has been awakened.

BODHI TREE   Pipal tree under which Shakyamuni Buddha experienced enlightenment after many years of determined practice.

BODHIDHARMA   Known as the First Ancestor, Bodhidharma brought Zen to China from India. He is said to have met Emperor Wu, who failed to appreciate his teachings, and then retreated to a cave where he did *zazen* for nine years. He transmitted to the Second Patriarch, Hui-k'o (Jap. Eka). Bodhidharma is associated with the well-known verse:

A special transmission outside the scriptures
No dependence on words and letters.
Seeing directly into the human mind
Realizing true nature, becoming Buddha.

BODHISATTVA One who practices the Buddha Way and compassionately postpones final enlightenment for the sake of others; the ideal of practice in Mahayana Buddhism.

BUDDHA HALL Traditionally, the room or building in a Zen Buddhist monastery in which services are held.

BUDDHA WAY The practice of realization taught by Shakyamuni Buddha.

DHARMA The word sometimes means Buddhist teachings, at times refers to all phenomena, and also means universal, ultimate truth.

DHARMA COMBAT Unrehearsed dialogue in which two Zen practitioners test and sharpen their understanding of Zen truths.

DHARMA DISCOURSE Formal talk given by a teacher explicating a koan. Not a philosophical explanation, but a direct expression of the spirit of Zen which speaks to that spirit in the listener.

DIAMOND NET OF INDRA Image from the *Avatamsaka Sutra* of the Hua-yen school of Buddhism, pictured as a net with a jewel at each intersection. Each jewel reflects every other, graphically demonstrating the simultaneous mutual interdependence and intercausality of all things. See *Hua-yen.*

DOGEN KIGEN ZENJI (1200–1253) Founder of the Japanese Soto school of Zen, Dogen established Eiheiji, the principal Soto training monastery of Japan. He is the author of the *Shobogenzo,* an important collection of Dharma essays. See *Shobogenzo.*

GLOSSARY

DUKKHA The First Noble Truth taught by Shakyamuni Buddha. Often translated as "suffering," it means, more widely, the unsatisfactoriness of human life. Dukkha is said to originate from desire, or grasping. See *Four Noble Truths; Nirodha.*

EIGHTFOLD PATH The path that leads to liberation, consisting of right understanding, right aim, right speech, right action, right livelihood, right effort, right mindfulness, and right concentration.

ENLIGHTENMENT The direct experience of one's true nature.

FAITH MIND SUTRA Sutra on nonduality composed by the Third Ancestor of Zen, Seng-ts'an (Jap. Sosan, d. 606).

FOUR BODHISATTVA VOWS "Sentient beings are numberless; I vow to save them. Desires are inexhaustible; I vow to put an end to them. The Dharmas are boundless; I vow to master them. The Buddha Way is unsurpassable; I vow to attain it." Chanted daily by Zen students as an expression of their aspiration.

FOUR NOBLE TRUTHS One of the earliest and most fundamental teachings of Shakyamuni Buddha concerning human life and the Buddha Way. They are: (1) life is suffering *(dukkha);* (2) suffering has a cause; (3) there is a way to put an end to the cause of suffering; (4) the way to put an end to the cause of suffering is the Eightfold Path. See *Dukkha; Nirodha.*

GATELESS GATE *(Mumonkan)* A collection of forty-eight koans compiled, with commentary and appreciatory verse, by Wu-men Hu-k'ai (Jap. Mumon Ekai) in the thirteenth century.

GENJOKOAN "Realization of Ultimate Reality" or "The Way of Everyday Life," one of the key chapters of Dogen Zenji's *Shobogenzo.* An important Soto Zen text, it subtly explores the relationship between practice and realization.

HARA The center of gravity of the body, located in the lower abdomen; the center of awareness in *zazen.*

HEART SUTRA   A distillation of the vast *Prajnaparamita* literature, it is chanted daily in Zen monasteries.

HINAYANA ("Lesser Vehicle")   The Southern School of Buddhism, from which Mahayana Buddhism evolved. See *Theravada.*

HUA-YEN   Chinese school of Buddhism, founded in the seventh century, which attempted a synthesis of all the major schools, texts, and traditions of the time. The teachings of mutual interdependence and mutual causality are hallmarks of the school. See *Diamond Net of Indra.*

KALPA   An eon; an extremely long period of time; incalculable time.

KENSHO   "Seeing into one's own nature"; first experience of realization.

KOAN   An apparently paradoxical anecdote or story. Koans are used to bring Zen students to realization and to help clarify their enlightenment. Approximately seventeen hundred koans have been recorded from Chinese and Japanese sources. They can be found in various collections, most notably *The Gateless Gate, The Blue Cliff Record* and *The Book of Equanimity.* See *Blue Cliff Record; Gateless Gate.*

MAHAKASHYAPA   The dharma heir and most prominent disciple of Shakyamuni Buddha. The First Ancestor in the Zen tradition, he was responsible for convening the first Buddhist council after the death of the Buddha.

MAHAYANA ("Great Vehicle")   The Northern School of Buddhism, which developed some centuries after the death of Shakyamuni Buddha. It emphasizes compassion for all sentient beings; the Bodhisattva, who works tirelessly for the benefit of all, is the model for practice. See *Bodhisattva.*

MAGGA   Path, or way.

MAKYO   Fantasies, hallucinations, and seemingly real mental or physical experiences that arise during zazen; they are an obstacle to practice.

MANJUSHRI   One of the principal Bodhisattvas of the Zen Buddhist tradition. Manjushri personifies wisdom and is often represented riding a lion and holding the sword of wisdom, which can cut through delusion. Also known as Monju in Japanese.

MOUNT GUDHAKUTRA Vulture Peak, the site of many of Shakyamuni Buddha's recorded discourses and important in Zen as the site of the first transmission from the Buddha to Mahakashyapa. See *Mahakashyapa.*

MOUNTAINS AND RIVERS SUTRA Fascicle in Dogen Zenji's master work, the *Shobogenzo.*

MU Often the first koan of the beginning Zen student. Mu has no intrinsic verbal meaning and cannot be penetrated by discursive thought. The koan originated with Chao-chou Ts'ung-shen (Jap. Joshu Jushin, 778–897), who, when asked by a monk, "Does a dog have Buddha nature?," directly answered, "Mu!"

NIRODHA The end to ignorance, which causes suffering; the Third Noble Truth taught by Shakyamuni Buddha. See *Dukkha; Four Noble Truths.*

NIRVANA A nondualistic state beyond life and death; extinction of attachment to desire and delusion.

OBAKU ZEN School of Zen brought from China to Japan in 1654 by Yin-Yuan (Jap. Ingen). Obaku was the teacher of Rinzai, the founder of the Rinzai school of Zen.

PARAMITAS In Mahayana Buddhism, the six perfections practiced by Bodhisattvas. The paramitas include wisdom *(prajna)*, patience *(kshanti)*, generosity *(dana)*, meditative awareness *(dhyana)*, effort *(virya)*, and precepts *(sila)*. Four more are sometimes included: skillful means *(upaya)*, determination *(pranidhana)*, strength *(bala)*, and knowledge *(jnana)*. See *Bodhisattva.*

PRAJNA Wisdom or insight of enlightenment; nondiscriminating awareness.

PRECEPTS Buddhist ethical teachings that directly point to reality. At *jukai*, the ceremony of becoming a Buddhist, Zen students make a commitment to maintain the precepts. The precepts are: the Three Treasures (be one with the Buddha, be one with the Dharma, be one with the Sangha), the Three Pure Precepts (do not commit evil, do good, do good for others), the Ten Grave Precepts (do not kill, do not steal, do not be greedy, do not lie, do not be ignorant, do not talk about others' faults, do not elevate yourself by criticizing others, do not be stingy, do not get angry, do not speak ill of the Three Treasures).

SAMADHI   Mental state characterized by concentration and one-pointed attention; a nondualistic state of awareness.

SANGHA   Traditionally, the monastic order; in a broader sense, the Sangha includes all Buddhist practitioners. In Zen, the term also connotes the harmonious interrelationship of all beings, phenomena, and events.

SHAKYAMUNI   The historical Buddha.

SHIKANTAZA   "Just sitting"; zazen itself, without the usual techniques of koan study or breath counting; a state of deep, nondiscriminatory awareness.

SHOBOGENZO ("Treasury of the True Dharma Eye")   The masterwork of Dogen Zenji, this work is made up of ninety-five fascicles on Buddhist subjects and is considered a milestone in Buddhist literature. See *Dogen Kigen Zenji.*

SKANDHAS   The five impermanent components of human mind: form, sensation, conception, discrimination, and awareness. Together they give rise to the illusion of a permanent, separate self.

SOTO ZEN   School of Zen originating in China with Tung-shan Liang-chieh (Jap. Tozan Ryokai, 807–869) and Ts'ao-shan Pen-chi (Jap. Sozan Honjaku, 840–901). Dogen Zenji brought the Soto lineage to Japan, cofounding the Japanese school with Keizan Jokin Zenji (1268–1325).

SUMI-E   Japanese brush-and-ink painting associated with Zen practice, characterized by rapid, spontaneous strokes.

SUTRA   Important Buddhist texts or scriptures containing the teachings of Buddhism. Sutras often record the words attributed to Shakyamuni Buddha or later masters.

GLOSSARY

TEN OXHERDING PICTURES   Traditional images that depict the stages of Zen practice. The pictures begin with the stage of searching for the ox, in which the desire to practice is awakened, and end with the return to the marketplace, in which the practitioner functions freely and compassionately in the world.

TOKUDO   Ordination as a trainee for the priesthood.

THERAVADA ("Way of the Elders")   The Southern School of Buddhism, emphasizing individual practice and attainment. The central institution is the Sangha, or monastic order, and the taking of the Three Refuges (Buddha, Dharma, and Sangha) is basic to the practice.

TRANSMISSION OF THE LAMP   A record of the lives and sayings of Zen masters from the earliest days to the tenth century, compiled in 1004 by Tao-yuan.

VIMALAKIRTI   A lay contemporary of the Buddha, whose spiritual attainment is highly regarded. He exemplifies the Mahayana model of fully realized nonmonastic practice. The *Vimalakirti Sutra* contains his teachings.

ZAZEN   "Sitting zen," the formal practice of breath counting, koan study, or shikantaza.

ZENDO   The space in a monastery in which zazen is practiced; it is often set aside exclusively for this purpose.

ZUISE   A special empowerment ceremony currently held only at the temples of Eiheiji and Sojiji in Japan by new priests upon reaching the priestly rank.

ABOUT
ZEN MOUNTAIN
MONASTERY

ZEN MOUNTAIN MONASTERY is an American Zen Buddhist monastery and training center for monks, nuns, and lay practitioners. Located on a 200-acre site surrounded by thousands of acres of state forest wilderness preserve on Tremper Mountain in New York State's Catskill Mountains, the monastery provides a year-round daily training program that includes Zen meditation, face-to-face teaching, Dharma Talks, liturgy, work practice, body practice, and art practice. Each month a week-long, silent Zen meditation retreat *(sesshin)* is offered. During the spring and fall quarter of each year, ninety-day Zen training intensives are conducted. During the summer quarter, the regular schedule is supplemented with seminars and workshops in the Zen arts and Buddhist studies. Students train in either full-time or part-time residency or as nonresident students whose "at-home" training is supplemented by periodic visits to the monastery. For further information, contact:

REGISTRAR
ZEN MOUNTAIN MONASTERY
P.O. BOX 197DC
MT. TREMPER, NY 12457

INDEX

Aikido, 10

American, Zen, xi, xiv; Zen masters, xi, xiv; Zen students, xi, xiv, 152–153

Ananda, and the Buddha, 113–114; and transmission from Mahakashyapa, 112–113, 116, 118–119, 121

anger, 160; *see also* separation; three poisons

anuttara samyak sambodhi, 103, 108, 117

art, and creative audience, 177; and Kamakura Japan, 127; and religion, 94; and Zen practice, xvii, 8, 10, 94, 127–128, 169

asceticism, 13, 152

aspiration, 21–22; *see also* bodhi-mind; determination

attachment. *See* greed; three poisons

Avolokiteshvara, 32–33

barriers, 8, 15–16, 19

Basho Pond, 45

Baso, Master, and Bodhidharma, 96; and Nansen, 142

Blue Cliff Record, x, xvi, 74, 93–94

Bodhidharma, and determination, 199; coming from the West, 142–143; and Second Ancestor, 16, 18, 98; and Sozan, 158

bodhi-mind, 12, 13, 20, 48, 52

Bodhi Tree, 13, 117

Book of Equanimity, x, xvi

breath, 48; *see also* zazen

Buddha, and adapting to circumstances, 148; and asceticism, 152; and ceaseless practice, 48; and freedom, 58, 87; Gautama's eyeballs, 130–131; as healer, 147; image, 194; and lineage, xiv; and makyo, 151–152; and realization, x, 52–59, 78, 94, 117, 199; and self and no-self, 22, 85, 89, 107, 172, 199; and the spiritual search, 7; and suffering, 8, 73; and transmission, 48, 65, 98, 113, 154; words of the, 13, 32

Buddhadharma, 89, 167–168, 172

Buddha-mind, xiv, xvii, 38

Buddha Way, xvi, 8

Buddhism, and academic study, 155; and attachment, 97; historians, 90; psychology, 86–87; and reality, 86, 104; and self, 44; and the spiritual search, 8, 18. *See also* Hinayana, Mahayana

Buji, Zen. *See* Zen

Catholicism, x, 8, 21

cause and effect, 54, 57, 150

China, xi; language and Zen literature, 33, 66, 127; and the Golden Age of Zen, 90; and the spiritual search, 7; and the Sung Dynasty,

213

10; and the Third Patriarch, 158
Chinese Zen masters, xiv, 194
Christ, 7, 112
Christianity, 18, 111–112
Chizo, 142
compassion, 20, 48–49, 105
consciousness, Buddhist psychology and, 86–87; and intuition, 2; linear thought, 2, 114–115; and moment-to-moment awareness, 95
conditioning, 12, 18, 21, 42, 77, 105, 180, 188, 196

desire, 42–43, 105; see also greed, separation
determination, 4, 12, 23, 188. See also aspiration, bodhi-mind, faith
Dharma, xi, xiv, xv
Dharma Combat, 9, 146
Dharma Discourse, xiii, xvi, 2, 4, 9
Dhyana, 104
Diamond Net of Indra, 158, 161–162; see also Hua-yen philosophy
Diamond Sutra, 86, 98
Dogen Zenji, and cause and effect, 55; and ceaseless practice, 49; and intimacy, 63–64, 74, 94–95, 125–128; as a monk, 49; and six prajnas, 103–105; reality, 48, 61–62; the secular and the sacred, 70, 108, 167, 172–173; and self study, 15, 107, 120; Shobogenzo, x, xv, xvi, 47, 104, 126, 130–131; and suffering, 105; as a teacher, 15, 47, 115, 131
Doshinji, 8, 10, 50, 127
doubt, xv, 4, 12, 19, 188
dualism, 151, 197
duality, 159
dukkha. See suffering, Four Noble Truths

Eightfold Path, 105
Eiheji, x, 15
Eka, 98; see also Second Ancestor
emptiness, 35–36, 150
Engo, Master, 70–73, 77, 92, 95, 193
enlightenment, x, xvi, xvii, 48, 97, 108, 111, 114, 119, 120, 148, 152, 162, 196
Eno, Master, 14

faith, 4, 12, 158, 188
Faith Mind Sutra, 157–158
Four Bodhisattva Vows, 143
Four Noble Truths, 45, 104; see also suffering
Four Positions, 139
Francis of Assisi, 18
freedom, 29, 47, 77–78, 137, 190, 196. See also Zen and freedom
Fuller, Buckminster, 44

Gateless Gate, The, x, xvi, 41, 44
Gautama. See Buddha
Genjokoan, 126; see also Dogen Zenji; Shobogenzo
golden chain. See precepts
Great Determination. See determination
Great Doubt. See doubt
Great Faith. See faith
greed, 20, 44, 97. See also three poisons
Gyokusei Jikikhara Sensei, 7, 10

Han Shan, 66
hara, 9, 176
Heart Sutra, xvi, 31, 106, 108, 195
Hinayana, 83–85; see also Theravada Buddhism
Hinduism, 8, 111–112
Hogen, 126

Hua-yen philosophy, 54
Hyakujo, Master, 142

Ichu, 127–128
India, xi, 9
Intimacy, 126; see also Dogen and
   intimacy
intensive training period, 9
interview (dokusan), 9, 75
intuition, 196; see also consciousness
Iron Grindstone Liu, 90
Isan, Master, 90
Islam, 111

Japan, x, 1, 131
Japanese, xiv, xv, 127
Jesus, 147; see also Nazarene
Jikihara Sensei. See Gyokusei Jiki-
   hara Sensei
Jizo, 126
Jo, Master, 96
John of the Cross, 18
Johoshi, 93
joriki, 187
Joshu, Master, 115, 142; Faith
   Mind Sutra, 160–162; and Nan-
   sen, 53, 172
Judaism, 111–112

Kakuan, Master, 7–8, 12
Kamakura (period in Japan), 10,
   127
Kashyapa. See Mahakashyapa
Karate, 10, 195, 197–199
karma, 13, 43, 129, 139, 163
Keizan, Master, 117, 119, 121
kensho, 188–189; see also enlightenment
kesa, the verse of the, 118
koan, collections, xiv, 1, 3; and determination, 188; and dharma
   discourse, xiv; of everyday life,
   170–171; and faith and doubt, 4,

188; and intuition and intellect,
   1, 2, 3, 4, 15, 17, 182; and Sho-
   bogenzo, 131; and zazen, 3, 29;
   Zen training, xv, xvi, 2, 3
Kung Fu, iv
Kyogen, Master, 142
Kyosei, Master, 69–76

laymen, xv, xvi, 136
Ling Chao (daughter of Layman
   P'ang), 135–136, 140–143
liturgy (and Zen practice), xvii, 8–
   10

Machaku, 33, 193–195, 200
Maezumi Roshi, 62
magga, 105
Mahakashyapa, enlightenment of,
   98, 114, 117, 154; transmission to
   Ananda, 112, 119
Mahayana, 82–86
makyo, 151–152
Manjushri, 82–83, 149, 193–194,
   200
martial arts, 9, 10; see also, Aikido,
   Karate, Kung Fu
Matsu, Master, 136
meditation, as core of practice, 9; as
   sickness, 148. See also zazen
monastery, x, xi; Dogen and
   monastic rules, 50; as a sanctuary
   and furnace, 167; see also Zen
   Mountain Monastery
monks, American Zen, xv; ancient
   monks and danger, 18; Dogen as,
   49
Moses, 7, 147
Mountains and Rivers Sutra, 63, 65;
   see also Dogen Zenji
Mount Gorba, 194
Mount Gudhakutra, 114, 119, 121,
   129, 154
Mount Ko, 66

Mount Sumeru, 142
Muchaku, 194
Muhammad, 7; *see also* Islam
Mumon, Master, 44
Myozen, 90
mysticism, 18, 51

Nambutzu, 127–128
Nansen, Master, 95, 97, 100; and
    Joshu, 53, 93, 96; and Taifu, 96,
    98
Nazarene, 62, 65; *see also* Jesus,
    Christianity
Nenga, 10, 19
nirodha (the truth of suffering),
    105; *see also* suffering
nirvana, 37, 48, 52. *See also* enlight-
    enment

Obaku (Zen sect), 10
Oxherding Pictures, 7, 8, 120

P'ang, Layman, xvi, 135–136, 140,
    143, 172. *See also* Lin Chao
paramita, dana paramita, 107; pra-
    jna paramita, 107; six paramitas,
    33
Perfection of Wisdom Sutra, 32
"Plum Blossoms," 138; *see also*
    Dogen Zenji, Shobogenzo
poetry, 94
pointer (for koans), x, xvi, 3, 137
practice, ceaseless, 48, 52; and com-
    mitment, 19; as doing, xvi, 2, 8,
    9, 11, 168; and enlightenment,
    108; and flexibility, 153; as grati-
    tude, 13; and koans, x, xi, 2;
    nonresident, 12; and reality, 49;
    and self, 107–109; stages of, xv,
    9, 50–51; and trust, 163; work,
    xvii, 8, 167–172
prajna, 33, 103; *see also* Dogen and
    prajnas
precepts, 107

questions (and answers in Zen train-
    ing), 17, 115

realization, and belief, 22; and Bud-
    dha nature, 13; and conditioning,
    86; and intellectual understand-
    ing, 1, 2, 115; and practice, 1, 52,
    155; and the self, 45, 86
reality, 1, 3, 18, 49, 86, 121, 149,
    160; *see also* enlightenment
responsibility, and practice, 43, 71,
    149–150; and realization, 189;
    and reality, 98; and separation,
    77; and wisdom, 108
Rikyu Taifu, 93, 95–98, 100
Rinzai, Master, 21, 44, 72, 115
Rinzai (school), xv, 131
ripeness, 117–118
rohatsu, 198
Russians, 44

samadhi, 9, 187–188
samsara, 155
samurai, 127, 198
Sanskrit, 32
satori, 21; *see also* enlightenment
Scully (Monsignor), 62
Second Ancestor, 17, 98; *see also*
    Eka
seeing, 99, 175–177, 181
self, 16, 37, 43, 77, 94, 97, 163, 185
separation (and no separation), and
    barriers, 138; and ceaseless prac-
    tice, 48; and communication, 75;
    and compassion, 34; and Di-
    amond Net of Indra, 158, 160–
    161; and doing, 20; and freedom,
    56, 144; and *Heart Sutra,* 37,
    106–107; and koan study, 188;
    and *Mountains and Rivers Sutra,*
    63, 65; and prajna, 33; and
    realization, 12; and responsibility,
    88; and seeing, 181; and stress,
    184; and suffering, 73; and the

three poisons, 73; and Zen, 97, 185

sesshin, 9

Seppo, Master, 70

Setcho, Master, 53, 100, 154, 194, 200

Shakyamuni Buddha. *See* Buddha

Shariputra, 32, 81–87

Shibayama, Master, 19

shikantaza, x, 29

Shobogenzo, 50, 126, 131; *see also* Dogen

Sholin Monastery, 10

sila, 107

skandas, 34

Soto (school), and Dogen, 61; and Eiheji, 15; and koans, 131; lineage, xv; monasteries, x

Sozan, Master, 157–158, 160, 163

stress, 183–184

Sudhana, 147

suffering, 47, 50–51, 73, 104

sumi-e, 169

Sung (Dynasty in China), 10

sutras, x

Sutra of the Third Patriarch, 140

Su T'ung-Po, Master, 64–65

Taifu. *See* Rikyu Taifu

Tang (Dynasty in China), 96

Tao, 172

Ta-yang, Master, 61

Tendo Nyojo, 128–129, 131–132

Theravada Buddhism, 119; *see also* Hinayana

Theresa of Avila, 18

Third Noble Truth. *See* Four Noble truths, suffering

Third Patriarch, 140, 157–158. *See also* Sozan

three poisons, 12, 73; *see also* anger, greed

Three Treasures, 138; *see also* Buddha, dharma, sangha

Tokusan, Master, 70, 72, 76

training (Zen), and ability, 11; as doing, 2; and sesshin, 9; at ZMM, xvi, 10–11

transmission, xi, xiv, 1, 77, 98, 111

Transmission of the Lamp, xvi, 17, 111, 121

Treasury of the True Dharma Eye. See Shobogenzo

truth. *See* reality

Unmon, 74, 115, 147–149

verse (for koans), x, xvi, 3

Vimalakirti, 82–84, 90

Way of Everyday Life, The, 62

women, 90, 135, 140–141, 198

Yasutani Roshi, 130, 139

zazen, as activity, 168; and beginning practice, xv, 9; and breath, 25, 27, 28; and concentration, 25, 28, 187; and enlightenment, 1, 25; and letting go, 190; and makyo, 151–152; physical arrangements for, 2–5; and posture, 25–26; and stillness, 185–186; and thoughts and emotions, 26–28; at ZMM, xviii, 7

Zen, and academic study, xiv, xvii, 8–9; and aceticism, 152; as activity, 11, 13, 188–189; and art practice, 10, 12, 94, 169; and belief, 77–78; Buji, 155; and despair, 29; and helping, 19; and freedom, 29; and koans, xv, 1; and meditation, 8; and monasticism, xv; and motivations for, 15;

and patience, 29; and psychotherapy, 22; and romance, 12; and responsibility, 41; and seamlessness, 50, 52; and separation, 185; and stages of training, xv, 9, 88–89; and stillness, 195; teachers, xviii, 3, 4, 111, 115; and time, 129, 150; uniqueness of, 9, 111–112

zendo, 9
zenga (painting), 169
Zen Mountain Monastery, x, xiii, xv, 7–8, 50, 119
Zenshuji, ix
Zuigan, Master, 41–42, 44, 74
zuisse, x